# How to Become an Escape Artist

## A Traveler's Handbook

# How to Become an Escape Artist

## A Traveler's Handbook

**Jackie Chase**

www.AdventureTravelPress.com

*How to Become an Escape Artist: A Traveler's Handbook*
By Jackie Chase

*AdventureTravelPress.com, Lady Lake, FL 32159*


*How to Become an Escape Artist: A Traveler's Handbook*
By Jackie Chase
Color Print: ISBN- 978-1-937630-18-8
E-book: ISBN- 978-1-937630-14-0
******Grayscale Print: ISBN 978-1-937630-22-5***
www.JackieChase.com; www.CulturesOfTheWorld.com

Publisher's Cataloging-In-Publication Data
(Prepared by The Donohue Group, Inc.)

Names: Chase, Jackie, author, photographer.
Title: How to become an escape artist : a traveler's handbook 2nd Ed. / Jackie Chase.
Description: FL, USA : AdventureTravelPress.com, [2016]
Identifiers: LCCN 2014935897 | ISBN 978-1-937630-22-5 (grayscale print) | ISBN 978-1-937630-18-8 (color print) | ISBN 978-1-937630-14-0 (ebook)
Subjects: LCSH: Travel--Handbooks, manuals, etc. | Tourism--Handbooks, manuals, etc.
Classification: LCC G151 .C43 2016 (print) | LCC G151 (ebook) | DDC 910.2/02--dc23

Contents

## About "Escape": Contains: 192 Sections; 113 Live Links; Endless Tips

The world is for you to experience, provided you have the courage and the tools to take a chance on trying new ideas and visiting new places.

Every journey begins with a single step, but every plan to travel begins with a dream. And this book is about making the dream for your travel experience unforgettable, so you will wish to continue your exploration to many parts of the world for business and pleasure.

The hints and ideas arise from a lifetime of travel by Jackie Chase, blogger at www.JackieChase.com who, in visiting over 100 countries, has used a blend of comfort (such as accommodations with US quality standards) and challenging situations (sometimes helping her to appreciate the extra care the hospitality industry offers by Western standards) in order to meet people in addition to merely seeing the basic sights.

You can read these hints in order, or use the contents pages to review them before, during, and after your trip.

Be sure to start dreaming by doing your reading and research as outlined in the following pages. And don't forget to help the dreams of your fellow globe mates by exploring ways to help through a wide variety of non-governmental charities and organizations, some of which are supported by a quality hotel system as listed below. A portion of the sales price of this book is set aside for "giving back" to those cultures that made this book and the author's other books interesting and mind expanding.

Please enjoy this unique Traveler's Handbook, and let the author know if you have any comments or suggested additions for the next printing.

# Introduction

In the process of growing up, we sometimes exchange reality for our youthful dreams of the exotic wonders of the world, including mysterious peoples. People face social and financial responsibilities that no doubt dampen their appetite for adventure. Have some folks sacrificed too much with this exchange? Can we retrieve our dreams?

Does something pull and tug at you that you cannot describe? Is there a "wannabe" adventurer inside you, bursting to get out? Do you long for a recess from your nine-to-five habit? The human imagination wants the freedom to take a journey into the unknown. Clouded memories of strangers or fast-paced sightseeing and a T-shirt in your closet linger as remnants of your last vacation. Months later, emotionally and physically, you have not changed. Shifting gears to adopt the life of an adventurer can transform your life in a permanent way. A new perspective remains long after your physical return.

Year after year, travel agents expect clients to call and book the same vacation again. These calls eliminate stress, effort, or fear of the unknown for most travelers. There is no need to step outside their comfort zones. Their expectations remain the same, and they avoid the challenges and risks in adventure travel when booking a typical tour-group vacation. Waiters and guides protect and take care of tourists, but if a traveler will leave a few hours available for exploration, the information in the following pages can provide solid strategies and encouragement to break from the norm for a few hours and observe the exciting local culture. Travelers who adopt the tips and the philosophy expressed here, can stretch those hours into a few more days on the next trip as a result of their new-found taste of adventure! The book contains the basic help every traveler needs, whether taking vacation days before or after a business trip or planning a family or personal vacation. You will not choose a right or wrong destination, for each has fascinating people and culture in and around your hotel, and we hope to help you see and appreciate those culture, rather than miss them completely.

Each trip should have some treats where we feel spoiled and some challenges where we stretch our curiosity for a memorable contact with a person or village different from our comfort zone.

This book urges each guest of a new culture to travel and keep traveling, for the more memorable each trip, the sooner you will wish to begin another. But the book should help in a positive way to seek out new experiences and to seek them in a way that can help prevent mistakes over time or money or missed opportunities.

As an experienced traveler, the author is able to find new places to see with a flexible schedule during the days allotted for the trip. But as a word of caution, when you arrive, take time to stay in a trusted hotel, so you can gather your courage after a long flight, and get acquainted with the customs, language, currency and local culture. Do the same before departing, by staying at a comfortable hotel so you arrive home happy and rested.

Adventurers do not need to budget a lot of money for their adventure excursions, nor should old age keep them from their dreams. You don't need to use aging as an excuse to avoid travel. Watch how "seasoned citizens" and travelers with disabilities cope with challenges! Come with a positive attitude, a sense of humor, and considerable patience. These traits will prepare you for any situation that arises and will help you learn from disappointments. This mixture will turn into magic, and, used with appropriate common sense, will help keep you safe, and help you maintain a balanced attitude.

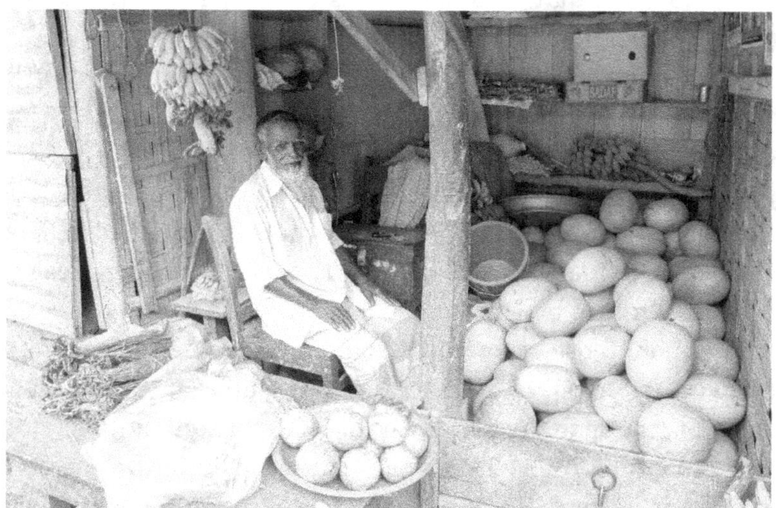

*1.Remote Thancy man selling melons, Bangladesh*

Why would you choose to leave the cushions of your home, use hard-earned money, and spend hours to travel to a foreign place? Why look for the enchantment of peculiar food, unfamiliar languages, and mysterious peoples living in unusual surroundings? As world villages condense, society accepts the interdependency between cultures. Doors open wide in every corner of the world for foreign visitors. Telecommunication opens the world in an instant, and air travel makes long-lost civilizations accessible in twenty-four hours. New neighbors live inside television sets and magazines, including those traditional peoples once lost in their own worlds.

Understanding other cultures is an important and often-discussed topic of our times. The relatedness of the world and ourselves excites our curiosity. Respect for the earth's people gives a traveler a richer life perspective. If we limit our exposure to photographs on computer screens, or to talk shows, which focus only on the crime or politics of other cultures, we miss a vital part of living.

As humans, we all have religion, family values, customs, and hobbies of music, art, and sports. Though the styles of music may differ, and the art, sports, and religions may differ as well, the fact that these things are important to all people around the world can bring us together as we meet with each other. To enjoy life and participate in the thrill of discovery, to walk into the unknown and find answers, we must uncover the truths about the world as we wander. The emotional journey that accompanies us along the way helps us to understand our inner selves.

Globetrotting may involve the challenge of unpredictable confrontations, and even the thought of this frightens many would-be travelers. However, as your eyes open to the realities of the world, you will fall in love with new and fulfilling risk-taking strengths that you never knew existed within yourself. Adventuring gives us the opportunity to try on new identities of self-confidence and independence, as we pay attention to our own capabilities. Seek an adventure, and you will return home changed in a profound way.

The unique and intense experiences you encounter will make a difference in the rest of your life. Do not let the demands scare you. Of course, you will have to invest in your emotional, physical, social, and spiritual nature before you set off on your adventure, as well as while you are away from the comfort and regularity of your normal life. But if you will let go of fear, you will observe first-hand the most amazing things surrounding you.

The word "travel" conjures images of sailing into romantic ports, climbing ancient ruins, or traipsing through wildlife-filled jungles. Our pockets contain dreams, and when we release those dreams, we can begin to enjoy them. When we let our spirits move us into uncharted territory, we have to depend on our instincts and judgment. Whether the reason to see the far corners of the world includes a desire to escape or to search out what we do not know, the challenge to deal with the unpredictable will await our commitment to act.

Motivation, more than logic or asking "why," moves and heightens the senses. Change into a chameleon. Reach out. Absorb. Awaken your senses with seeing, hearing, tasting, feeling, and smelling, and soon you will feel your spirit awakened. Open your life to foreign situations that scare you in the beginning. Make an effort to interact with the real people along the way. The more you encounter, the more you will want to confront, awakening instincts that forever long to see the excitement over the next hill.

As we begin to find our identity in every new situation, we expose our strengths and our weaknesses to strangers as well as to ourselves. Hundreds of lives, encountered along the way, share with us so many different examples of living. The world's characters improve our physical wellbeing and our spiritual and emotional selves. We discover within a philosopher and a poet, all because of the inconsistencies and simple ways of living we encounter.

This book seeks readers who want to make a commitment to escape, for an hour or a month, to reach for their dreams in an affordable and independent manner. The advice written here helps the traveler gather the courage to take that first leap. The information will not guarantee happiness or suggest the *when* and *where* of traveling, but it will seek to alter beliefs about global exploration. The information here will teach how to prepare and safeguard while living life on the road. It offers guidelines to inspire your intellect (or to whet your appetite for adventure), and to show how to deal with the vagaries of a journey. Most people have the courage and desire to travel to a faraway place. Lack of time, money, and layers of responsibility, cover those desires, making them difficult to bring to reality.

Traveling takes us on a journey into ourselves. For those wanting to travel with the author vicariously, the examples herein will guide the reader to various parts of the world. In addition, for those not quite ready for the unexpected in adventure travel, for those taking their first comfortable "tourist" trip to Europe, the hints offered here will aid in ALL travel situations, and give invaluable insights and suggestions.

# Chapter 1: tourist or independent traveler?

*"The road I chose became very much the road of life, and the ultimate qualification for inclusion was merely to have set foot on it."* Lisa St Aubin de Teran.

### *YOUR OPTIONS*

The words "intrepid," "fearless," and "brave" describe the modern traveler. Their confidence comes from achieving goals while knowing the world will help them fulfill their needs. Your reasons to travel will vary from those of other people, but you travel either as a tourist or an adventurer.

The tourist sometimes vacations with limited awareness of the culture around him or her. An adventurer looks for a richer life through travel. He uses his senses while discovering how other cultures survive. He experiences the history he spent hours researching before boarding his flight. To ride on the same camel which just returned from carrying salt for two weeks across the desert, or to handle the blowgun that just killed a cuscus for your dinner, or to pick spices that will taste like fire will expand the adventurer's knowledge of world cultures.

Locals put up with seeing tourists as a way to make money at typical tourist sites. An adventurer might take the time to earn respect and build relationships with local families who will, in turn, draw him or her into their lives. The adventurer might share a meal, earn an invitation to a special festival, or sleep in a villager's hut for a night. The adventurer seeks the unknown, drawn by the magnetic stimulation of travel, unusual peoples, places not found in glossy travel brochures, and simple, traditional ways of living.

Rewards of fulfillment come from initiating your own sojourn. Throughout my life, I have traveled in many disguises. As a mother, I taught my son how to bargain in the markets of Mexico. As a photographer, I captured my daughters with Maasai warriors, riding on the roof of a train in Ecuador and climbing the ruins of Tikal in Guatemala. As a writer, I recorded the antics of a 400-pound male orangutan in the jungles of Borneo. As a businessperson, I traveled as a courier to Seoul, Korea. As a backpacker, I trudged the jungles of New Guinea. As a student of world cultures, I tried to find the best way to travel within the countries I visited. I searched for the next episode of my life, sampling unfamiliar foods, and getting to know the people. Under specific conditions of travel, your best side will begin to emerge. For example, you may find joy in giving to others or strengthening the inner self.

As an independent traveler, you may wish, for a day or a week or two, to leave the take-for-granteds of Western society and step into the unknown. Observe how others live and view life, and you will receive the ultimate education.

We used to envision independent travelers as hippies or wandering college students with little money. Their image as undesirables came from modern First World attitudes. Things are so different now! College students from Western society often have more money than the people of the countries they visit. I have met a much greater diversity in independents when traveling, including men and women in their seventies, wealthy businesspersons out to gain a better understanding of their world, and homemakers on leave from their duties and now interacting with tribal women. Third and Fourth World countries welcome adventure travelers who provide a reliable source of income for the economy.

Independent travel includes traveling alone or with a couple of companions (maybe met on the way), making your own arrangements after you arrive. You involve yourself with the normal activities of the local people, which might include carrying water a mile in the desert from a well, pounding maize for dinner, smoking hand-rolled cigarettes with the local chief, or just listening as a group of young men play on handmade instruments. By making your own arrangements, you have the flexibility to evolve into a capricious traveler, taking advantage of unplanned situations that arise, and converting them to rich experiences. Exposure to the elements of weather, experiencing intense reactions to your arrival, unknown safety conditions, and unfamiliar food will teach tolerance, patience, and flexibility. Pack a sense of humor, often the primary means of retaining sanity.

The adventure traveler has many choices. There are times when, in a strange land, it is most comforting to see a friendly hotel system sign, where at the beginning middle and end of a trip, it feels great to be spoiled by the comforts of home. On a longer adventure trip, the first night or two in each strange city requires courage and a chance to assess all the new challenges. That sign, symbol of consistent quality and no surprises, is the perfect solution. But on your first adventure travel experience, please don't take the option of staying home because you fear the unknown. This book should give you the courage to do something different, and experience that once-in-a-lifetime discovery to share with your friends.

When taking a day or two to venture into the "back country", allow yourself a chance for submersion into the local culture. Accommodations range from small grass huts, a mosquito net hung from trees in the jungle, or a hammock slung high above insects on a sandy beach. Staying only at western style hotels is a comfortable option. But a day or two of "adventure" may lead to many new and exciting reasons to travel again, for in a luxury-only trip, there is something lost for the traveler in this type of arrangement: he often only interacts within his group, or if alone, with the interpreter, accustomed to constant dealings with foreigners and their money. He seldom, if ever, establishes a relationship with local people.

When on your own, you must approach locals. You will find yourself living and eating much in the same way they do. As a budget traveler from the First World, however, you will not have to live like the poor. Paying a small amount, sometimes in pennies, will give you a little cushion but still allow you to participate in the reality of the area. For example, instead of walking long distances, as the locals often do, you can travel by donkey cart through the sands of the Dogon country for a few extra dollars. While in Chiang Mai, take a rickshaw to the market instead of walking.

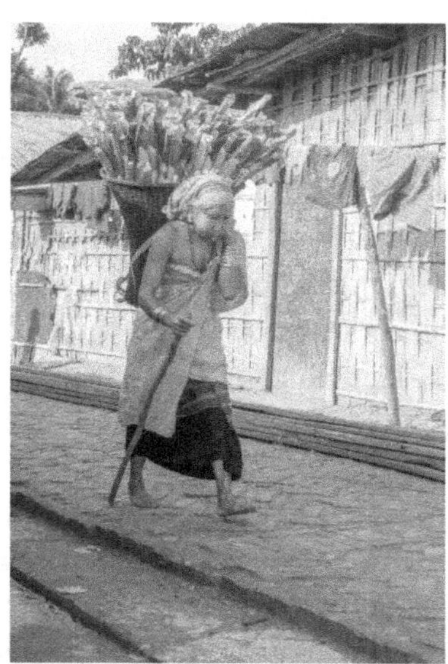

*2. Mru woman in Thancy, Bangladesh*

***WHICH WORLD DO YOU CHOOSE?***

Take courage! There are magnificent and unique accommodations in those 100 countries I have visited as well as primitive ones that helped me discover my strengths. You may wish to think about seeing a few of them. The North Atlantic Treaty Organization refers to the First World countries as capitalist and industrialized, with common political and economic interests. First World countries include the United States, Canada, Australia, New Zealand, Western Europe, Japan, and Singapore.

The term "Second World" originated during the Cold War, when the United States divided the entire world into our side and their side. The term now refers to the developed economies or former communist-socialist and industrialized countries of Russia, Eastern Europe, and China. Their tourist infrastructures and local costs remain common.

Countries with a capitalist, communist, mixed economy, or those trying to pursue independent economies could fall into the Third World country classification. Third World described the less-developed countries of Africa, Asia, and Latin America after World War II. Poor countries with unstable governments, high illiteracy, disease, and greater population growth fall into the Third World category. These countries have a high foreign debt and lack a middle class but have a large lower economic class and a small, wealthy upper class, managing the wealth and resources of the country.

Fourth World countries can fall into a category of not developing as an economic unit. The United Nations gave Fourth World countries the name "least developed countries" or LDC. Several countries carry this designation as long as they present three factors: 1). a per-person income of less than $905; 2). a human deficiency in nutrition, literacy, and health, and 3). vulnerability economically, including large numbers of populations uprooted by natural disasters. The places fitting these parameters include thirty-three African countries, nine Asian countries, five Oceania countries and one country in the Americas. These countries have the lowest economic and social development of all countries in the world.

Fourth World designations began in 1974, referring to ethnic groups living within or across country boundaries. These indigenous people often face discrimination. Geographers suggest using the terms LDC (Less Developed Country) or MDC (More Developed Country), and a broader generalization suggests using the terms *developed* and *developing*. No real standard exists in today's world.

Can we find differences between Third and Fourth World countries? Fourth Worlds lack infrastructure (basic installations or facilities like modern roads, communication systems, hotels, and public transportation). The Third World offers conveniences, like bottled water and packaged foods, flashlight batteries and film, all for a price.

Upon your return home, the spectacular sights you experienced abroad leave your memory banks faster than the face-to-face interaction with the native people you met, and the immediacy of living in their everyday worlds. These one-on-one, very personal encounters, create the glowing memories you will want to share with friends and family for years to come.

As humans, we ask questions and then find the answers. We desire to meet other people and to understand their ways of living, their customs, habits, what they eat, and how they work and play. We yearn to make a connection with someone new. Intrigued by the unfamiliar, we thirst for more knowledge and understanding. The traveler, while seeing the nature of things, gains a perspective of life different from the tourist's. Despite the cultural differences, he craves a close association with the people he meets. The more we learn about another country and the culture of its people, the more we learn about ourselves. As suggested earlier, the "adventure" ideas might fit inside a few hours of a guided tour, business trip, cruise, or vacation, and might lead to adventures that are more ambitious to dream about for the future. We come to know other cultures by connecting with them. How much can be gained by staying in their homes, sharing a meal with them, and taking part in their life and routines? So much! The rewards will come with patience, as native peoples might invite you to participate in their festivals once they get to know you better. They may arrange for locals to dance and play music for you. But this travel experience happens only when you allow time to go off on your own, and you will find it much easier to do this when traveling in a Third or Fourth World country. Traveling teaches you that people accept and trust outsiders with genuine open hearts.

Inexperienced travelers like staying in the First World, maybe going to Europe, enjoying landscapes and architecture. However, in a First World continent such as Europe, it takes far more creativity than in a Third World country to travel on a budget, interact with local people, and meet with challenging situations. It is only with difficulty in Europe that the traveler finds inexpensive food, and transportation. Guides and services cost more in European countries, and mistakes cost money. If the traveler pays fifty dollars for a train ticket and boards the wrong train, he cries. In a Third World country, the same distance may cost a few dollars and, so what, a new village awaits his arrival with new friends to meet, new foods to try.

In a Fourth World country, expect to see trains and buses in and around the capital cities. Your mode of transportation elsewhere takes advantage of local methods, such as camels, elephants, or dugout canoes, and transportation on these exotic conveyances cost only a few dollars! If your objective in visiting a country includes leaving the tourist traps behind, or experiencing how others live and how they view life, then mingling with locals in a poorer country holds more opportunities. These ideas may sound foolish or outside traditional personal boundaries. Consider them. Research and confidence will help make your dream trip come true. Do not deny yourself the opportunity.

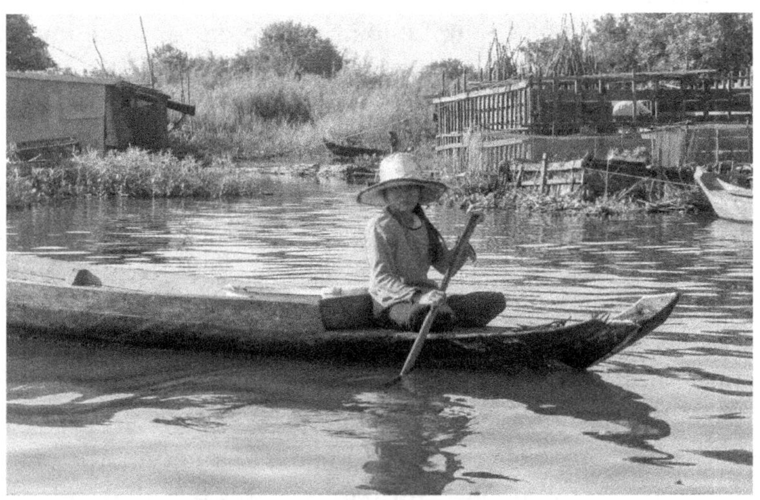

*3. Young girl going to market, Cambodia*

# chapter 2: leaving fear and careers behind

*"The world is a book and those who do not travel read only a page."*
St. Augustine

***PREPARATION***

Adventure travel calls for emotional and physical preparation. As others counsel us against the impractical side of daring adventure travels, they preach about the danger and expense of such a trip, or fret that you might lose progress in your job after a few weeks of absence.

Give yourself time to work through those thoughts of traveling alone, the dangers, and whether you will adjust to another culture. Avoid the trap of listening to advice that increases fear.

***BASIC NEEDS***

Many people fear leaving their basic needs of food, shelter, and security behind.

Traveling to places where the lifestyle we encounter deviates from the comforts of Western Society scares us. Replacing our reality with one unfamiliar to us requires adjustment even for the seasoned traveler. It is normal for us to be instinctively fearful of cultures we don't understand. Uneasiness and concern about travel diminishes with time on the road. Taking one small step at a time leads to larger steps and before you know it, you have built the confidence of a competent traveler.

***OBSTACLES***

We all face obstacles that challenge leaving our everyday routines. Children, businesses to operate, and school commitments tend to keep us from our pursuits of travel.

We also face these questions: Should we look at our value system and ask ourselves what we do and do not value now? Does fear of blazing a trail alone enter the picture?

Will our loyalty to our country's ways control our intentions, so that we cannot leave for a few days or weeks?

Alternatives abound if we prefer to look beyond organized tours that either remain outside our budget or which do not offer the mode of travel we prefer.

### *TRAVELING ALONE*

Human beings seek social contact with friends, relatives, crowds, or maybe just a pet dog. Leaving these comfortable relationships behind, whether traveling alone or with a group of strangers, your fears may surface. Traveling to another country means your reality of comforts and the well-known will change to the unfamiliar with strangers. Leaving at home those things you trust helps you find the courage to eat weird foods and experiment with new languages.

Traveling to find alone time can motivate you to plan for a trip. However, fear of loneliness accompanies you. Becoming lonely on a trip originates from many things: the relationships you left behind, your need to depend on others, the length of your trip, and your destination.

My experiences when traveling keep me so occupied, I seldom think of loneliness. Mysteries of international travel unfold each day. Just people-watching in an airport can open your eyes to a new way of looking at other cultures, observing how they dress, their body language, and their emotional reactions to the situations in which they find themselves. In some countries, just getting through the paperwork, customs, security and ticket agents (all in a foreign language) keeps you occupied. Time passes, while figuring out the why and how, while people-watching, helping with chores, or just absorbing the activities of life around you. Once you organize your thoughts and think about the next step, your confidence builds.

### *REMOVING MASKS*

Leaving home and the world (as we know it) changes us on that first flight. During the process of facing responsibilities on your own and meeting new people, you will reclaim inner thoughts, reactions, feelings, and decisions once thought lost. You will depend less on the routine actions expected of you by friends, spouse, or co-workers. You will have left your commercialized world. Soon, you will begin to feel alive! Our encounters with the unknown bring us out of the ruts we have fallen into as we reach a new level of awareness. We begin to see our new attitudes revealed. Released from society's boundaries, we anticipate liberation.

We wear predictable masks while we play our different roles. We do not speak our mind or share our wildest dreams for fear of others labeling us "crazy" or "outcast." Traveling opens the doors to honesty, making us outgoing and adventurous. We can let our guard down when we talk to strangers about ourselves because strangers offer a safety net. They will not judge us or disclose our information to people back home. We can talk about our real feelings without the fear of criticism, and remove our masks. If we act out of character, no unspoken rules (like those of home), come into play.

Immediate connections with other travelers thrive on buses, trains, hotels or even on street corners because they too have left their life of expectations behind, ready to face new challenges.

***FEAR OF OTHER CULTURES***

The unknown often cultivates fear. To overcome the fear of another culture, try to learn as much about the culture and its social behavior as possible. First-time travelers sometimes manage this fear with the attitude of demanding everything in the traditional, Western Society mode. They search for English-speaking guides, hotels where foreigners stay, and restaurants that cater to tourists. Although it is okay to travel this way, it restricts their ability to absorb the local culture. Encountering different customs often confuses and intimidates travelers. They do better to avoid diminishing the integrity of the culture by pretending that the differences do not exist. If they would but appreciate the differences of another culture, it would give them a feeling of immense joy. They are not required to accept or approve of the differences in order to observe them. By acknowledging social, political, and religious differences, they, as individuals, can build personal understandings of the great diversity of worldviews. One of the charms of sticking with ***western style*** hotels is their local flavor and ownership but predictable standards. You have heard of having your cake and eating it, too! That's an option to get you started into the excitement of adventure travel.

***FEAR OF FOREIGN LANGUAGES***

My friends often ask, "How do you travel to these places without speaking the local language?" Language barriers pose no problem for me. To prepare to communicate in a foreign language, I learn as much about the language as possible. A few essentials, such as hello and thank you, show respect toward the people I encounter while traveling. Sometimes I might find myself in such a remote area that languages differ from village to village. I have found that a guide of some sort can teach me the basic greetings. Keep in mind as you travel that you have a responsibility as a visitor. Figure out how to communicate with the culture you're visiting in a pleasant way. The most common foreign languages appear in phrase books available at bookstores and a serious reading of these guides before embarking on your trip will be invaluable to you.

If you find while abroad that you cannot remember certain important words or phrases, making motions of needing food or sleep will aid in communication. Drawing pictures of where you need to go works well too. One time in New Guinea, I did not want to trek uphill a lot. In order to explain this to my guide, I drew a picture of a mountain, used my fingers to indicate walking uphill, then shook my head and said no. He must have understood, as he picked me up on his back, carried me around the room, and said, "Okay, okay."

Not everyone will try to communicate with you. People of other cultures have the same fears as you. When lost, show someone a map, point to where you want to go, and if he shakes his head without even looking at the map, do not get mad. Respect his privacy and establish a warm contact with another local person.

New methods of technology make language translation so easy that travelers may take the lazy road to talking with locals. Electronic and book-form translation devices exist. Apps for your phone and tablet devices are easy to use and understand as long as you have Wi-Fi or cell service.

### *MEETING WITH THE UNEXPECTED*

Most people in a strange environment want to know as much as they can about their surroundings. We all figure out how to deal with the unfamiliar here at home from experience. You would not think of going on a ski trip for the first time without preparing. You do your research by asking friends, reading, and checking with businesses about what to take, where to rent equipment, and what to expect after arrival. As an independent traveler, you will have the same concerns about what you should expect. When traveling to a Third or Fourth World country, you have to prepare your emotions. Successful travel requires patience and flexibility. Frustrations occur with transportation delays, occasional boredom, strange-looking food, and unfamiliar faces. You need to tell yourself that you will not have the same control over new situations that you have at home. The conveniences of everyday life will not cushion your disappointments. For me, living without ice-cold drinks, taking cold showers or bathing in a river, and eating rice every day for weeks on end turned into a small sacrifice. But the upside of this was that I also had extraordinary experiences creating lasting connections with peoples of other cultures.

How might you handle the fear of feeling unqualified to meet with the unexpected? Educate yourself about your destination. Do as much research as possible before you go. Read travel narratives or anthologies from the library or bookstore. Many people now blog about their travel experiences, so don't overlook the wealth of knowledge you can pick up using your computer. Try to find stories about the area you plan to visit, and envision yourself in the shoes of travelers who have visited and written about those places. The simple act of asking directions can turn a stranger into a friend. You may find yourself invited for dinner with a local villager, one of the many advantages of independent travel.

### *WORDS OF ENCOURAGEMENT*

Sometimes we have to jump off the bridge and build our wings as we move forward in life. What holds you back? Will you waste time waiting for the right moment, that moment when you have just enough money, or a more stable job, and the children off in college? Take the time to reflect on the last several years. Count the things you accomplished. Realize your home world will remain intact while you are absent. You may find that your best side surfaces as your sojourn develops. As a traveler, your small risks will move you toward a richer life adventure.

### *CAREERS*

The majority of our lives we spend working, but we must stop and ask ourselves about our real goals. Traveling requires leaving our employment situation. Make an effort to forget about your guilt while you put your career on hold. Many of us spend too much time waiting for the right time to travel. We fear we will lose our positions or the work will pile up, so we keep trudging along, afraid to leave our jobs. Your job appears vulnerable when you travel, but, with planning, everything can remain stable.

How can you keep your flow of work uninterrupted while absent? It takes some skill, but you can spend some time organizing others to prepare for your absence. Long before your departure, begin by extending your workday and shortening your lunch break. Do your work in advance. Work ahead on projects, and recognize any deadlines coming up. Try to clear your desk before you leave. For those jobs needing to progress during your absence, figure out how to delegate responsibility to those helping you. What vacation standards exist elsewhere in the world? The standard paid European vacation includes four to six weeks away from work, and Swedes enjoy up to two months of freedom per year. Australians have four weeks of paid vacation plus a twelve-week service leave every ten to fifteen years. Why do Americans get one-third as much vacation time as Europeans and Aussies? If Americans knew this, we would see public protesting and a lot of hullabaloo. Most employers do not encourage recesses and discourage time off. Relieving stress, making new friends, and a change of scenery, could help to motivate us in all that we do (including work), and these periods of time off are necessary for recharging our batteries. Returning from a vacation rejuvenated and relaxed, we find our energy levels return to full steam (if only corporate America could understand that)! Many people spend far too much time working. Workaholics often miss the opportunity to enjoy living, trading good pay for a rich life. The benefits to your employer? Imagine returning with increased confidence, leadership abilities, and better time management!

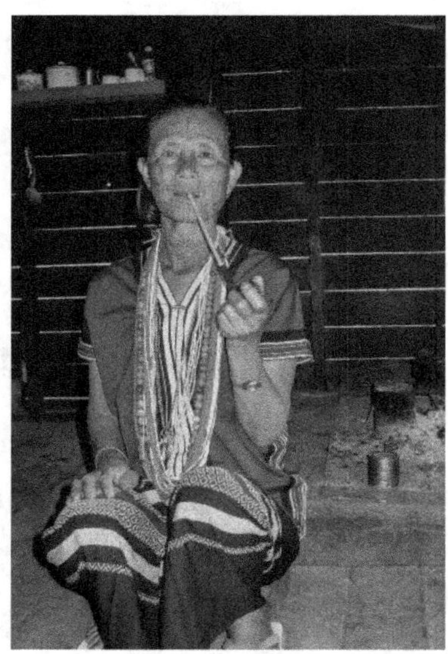

*4. Burmese woman with pipe*

# Chapter 3: the why and when to research

*"Two roads diverged in a wood, and I—I took the one less traveled by, and that has made all the difference."* Robert Frost

***TRAVELER TASTES/INTERESTS/PERSONALITIES***

What images and emotions enter your thoughts when they turn to the word "travel"? Thinking about the level of comfort and the tempo of activities you wish to have will help you decide on a travel plan. Every person has a different approach to travel and different requirements. Each of us needs to question what we can live with for the sake of adventure.

Imagine an environment involving fun and exploration. Now start the process of building your strategy toward making that place a destination. You can leave your training wheels on your bicycle, but you will never leave the sidewalk. It takes some modification to allow change in your life.

An adventure demands the energy and impulsiveness of a child. What you look for on your journey reflects your interests and personality. So, take the training wheels off your bicycle! The results of the challenge and the risks will reward you with personal growth.

***GATHERING IDEAS AND CHOOSING A DESTINATION***

Travel experiences range from sunning on some hidden island off the coast of Belize, to opening as many museum doors in a day in Paris as possible. Or they can include shaking hands with a tribal chief in Ethiopia, bouncing through the jungles of northern Thailand on elephants, and watching the magical marriage ceremonies of the Woodabe. Your choices of where and when will expand as you take your first step toward building your own adventure. Do key-chains, a splendid tan, or photographs some stranger took of you in front of the Eiffel Tower qualify as treasures of a trip? Or, are you more the type to seek the joy of discovery by expanding your knowledge of world events and developing an awareness of your own potential? Can you find the real magic of travel?

To bring about meaningful stimulation, intrigue, and beauty, we first need to clarify why and where. At a crossroad of decisions, we bring our ideas into focus. If you have no idea why you chose a certain path to travel, you may end up living someone else's ideas of what to do when you get there. These ideas include what sights to see, what foods to eat (or not to eat). You would forever look for experiences others suggest you "should" have, instead of exploring the places on your own terms.

***ANCESTORS***

Most Americans have ancestors from other countries. Maybe you have thought about trying to find more information about your ancestors' backgrounds, the historical events of your heritage, or the change in your relatives' culture over the years. Studying the language or the arts of your ancestors might help you to identify yourself. Perhaps you grew up with bits and pieces of your ancestors' language, and you have an affinity to learn more. Learning a language in the target country helps you notice the dialect and inflections. Learning more about your relatives' roots and how their culture may have influenced your own can change your life in a meaningful way.

***ALTERNATIVE TRAVEL***

What dreams do you have? Imagine unearthing a piece of an ancient ruin high in the Andes, documenting the habits of chameleons in Madagascar, developing an education program to help save the Leatherback Sea Turtles of Grenada, or watching for pandas in the Wolong Nature Reserve in China!

Consider exploring hundreds of untouched and unspoiled lands. Apply for a job as a field assistant in a land far away, helping scientists overcome obstacles in reaching their research goals.

Your determination, motivation, and perseverance will guide your actions as you live and work in conditions that can change in an instant due to capricious weather patterns and unexpected equipment breakdowns. Environmental vacations can offer low-impact travel, and an awareness of ecology. They help preserve the vulnerable ecological areas, and they ensure that the countries visited benefit as well.

To learn more about this kind of alternative travel, look for organizations specializing in low-impact or scientific study programs, world peace organizations, or universities offering research programs open to the public.

Meet like-minded individuals while volunteering or chasing after your interests.

### *RELAXATION*

Perhaps the word "travel" conjures images of sunning on a secluded beach in Bali, or bobbing up and down on the bow of a sailboat moving through Caribbean waters. Perhaps your idea of travel includes searching for pieces of sea glass, day after day, in the white sands of the Mediterranean. Think about it, and then take the time to plan your trip. Having just ten days and wanting to sail to every island in the Caribbean equates to a stressful vacation. Remember to travel off-season or you will face crowded beaches, overloaded buses, and noisy restaurants. Choose a location, and leave your calendar at home.

Workaholics suffering from severe "travelitis" can take work with them as they pursue their dreams. Let your creativity blossom. For example, if you happen to be an expert in the field of health, find a mission deep in the jungles of the Amazon, and teach your skills. If you sell products containing foreign materials, live with locals in that exporting country to gain a better understanding of what goes into the making of your products. Johnson Wax found Carnauba wax in South America with this open-minded approach. On the other hand, you could take a buying trip while attending an overseas trade show to enrich your own life experiences. The design of your trip may emphasize a special interest, such as cooking or hiking or both.

While trekking the 200-km-long Bandiagara escarpment, meeting with Dogon villagers in Mali, Africa, I had the opportunity to help with the preparation of vegetables cooked with different spices for my dinner, and I assisted in pounding millet for our porridge for breakfast. A Navajo woman living in a traditional *hogan*, herding sheep twice a day, taught me her ways of tapestry rugmaking with the wool she sheared, washed, and spun from her own sheep. If the urge to try an adventure trip overpowers all the above reasons for travel, then get your globe out and take a spin!

Finding the answer to the question "where?" should follow your research.

Do not choose a country, make all your plans to go there, and, after you arrive, find you have a strong negative feeling about the culture. Make sure you research the many facets of the culture before you set out: discover what foods will most likely be a staple in every home or offered at outside markets. Do you think you could handle a diet of raw octopus or broiled anteater? Would turning down food offered to you in hospitality cause a great problem? How should this be handled? What style of dress is appropriate for the culture? What style of dress will offend your hosts? And what about religious practices? Do you have enough understanding of the culture that you do not offend the religious sensibilities of the people? Some cultures you may find appealing and intriguing.

After arrival, some of their religious rituals could cause you discomfort. In Ethiopia, or any other Third or Fourth World country, committing a social taboo might cost you your life. At the very least, you might lose the privilege of staying in the village if you are not ready to follow the social norms or understand their expectations of you.

Let me give you a real-life example. Hidden deep in the forests of Ethiopia, I undressed for a quick wash at the local well. Suddenly, several young men (who were dressed in animal skins, their bodies painted with white designs), appeared beside me and proceeded to operate the handle on the well in order to draw water for themselves. I tried using hand motions to convince them to go away. At first, they stayed, and I ended up washing with my sarong on while they pumped water. After a few days of enduring me shooing at them, and my harsh commands that they go away while I bathed, they stopped coming to the well. I did not see them again, or anyone else from their village.

We left the village, and a week later, my guide admitted that the people there considered us rude, as the young boys had a duty to operate the well. This, my guide told me, was the reason he had arranged our departure from the village.

Expect unknown challenges as a female traveling alone. Solo travelers face unwanted attention, which means an awareness of surroundings is warranted. Women need to dress conservatively while ignoring whistles or inappropriate language given by bored men. In distressful situations, women need to shout for attention from others or make a scene.

Remember the importance of flexibility, patience, and open-mindedness, but consider, too, your own personal compatibility with local customs. Sometimes, there are things you will find you are unwilling to do, and that is all right. However, remember, you can also just let things happen, remaining flexible to whatever circumstances come your way, and (of course) alert to any dangers. Keep in mind that you took the trip to appreciate the differences between your culture and another culture.

In Ethiopia, my guide did not realize the importance of my need for coffee first thing in the morning. On this trip, I brought all my own food and a water purifier (found broken in checked luggage). I wanted Girma (my guide) to start a fire for me for boiling river water for coffee each morning. He would sit and talk with the local kids for an hour or more before even thinking about gathering firewood. He knew I needed the brown, muddy water boiled for at least thirty minutes, as a safety precaution. I tried to explain each morning about my need for caffeine.

After a few days, I realized all the incredible things I missed by sitting around and waiting for him to boil my water. I wandered the village, finding photo opportunities galore. After several days of my watching and smiling, I received invitations from locals to visit their huts. A group of women and young boys decided I had earned the privilege of wearing the brass bracelets adorning all females.

For two hours, the women bent and pounded with rocks the brass bracelets onto my arm, causing me numerous bruises and cuts. With pride, they gave me ten bracelets, bound to my left arm, a lasting memory of sharing their custom.

This tribe, called the Hamar, owned nothing but the animal skin clothing they wore. Some had shoes made from rubber tires. Yet they shared with me their most precious possession, the jewelry that defined their wealth. Had I continued to sit around my fire grumbling because Girma wasn't gathering firewood, I would have missed this precious experience!

One definition of intelligence emphasizes the ability to learn or understand and to cope with new situations. This ability summarizes the key to successful travel. The more you understand about transportation, food, shelter, and the lifestyle of the people you visit, the fewer hassles you will have, and the less money you will spend.

Planning for travel involves research, a pleasure in itself. It builds your anticipation before going, and rewards you with an easier trip along the way. Whether you travel to go canopy walking in Borneo or to photograph temples in Bangkok, your research creates the icing on your cake.

### *VOLUNTEERING*

The act of offering your enthusiasm and skills to others positively changes your life. Whether you volunteer to feel needed, to share your professional skills, to gain recognition from accomplishments, or just to escape is not important. Organizations all over the world need your help. Wanting to contribute is great, but it is even more satisfying to get something back from volunteering. Spend time researching for an organization that interests you. Work in an orphanage in Nepal, track the habitats of gorillas or cheetah in the bush, protect our ocean's precious ecosystem while diving in the Seychelles, teach children English all over the world, dive with dolphins in Fiji, or find construction projects even in your hometown. If you are the type who believes there is no better way to find happiness than to go out and find a cause and make a difference, do some research online with the subject of your interest. Some organizations charge a fee to help pay for your food and board. Check out sites like www.globalvolunteers.org or www.habitat.org.

.

***INTERNET***

The first place on your list of "to-goes" should include researching the internet. If you take the time to travel and spend hundreds of dollars on airfare getting there, wouldn't you want to take at least a full day searching for background information, comparing costs, and learning all the how-tos? You will find your anticipation building as you visit sites with beautiful photographs and well-written descriptions or reviews. The diversity and the number of choices can inspire you to keep looking. Try to narrow your search to a part of the world that appeals to you. Begin by taking notes. The State Department has helpful publications called "Background Notes" and "Post Reports." Do not avoid traveling because you have no expertise in the area of your interest. Start your research as soon as possible, not after you have decided on an area for travel. Your reward for researching before you go will benefit you before, during, and after your trip. Research will also help in your awareness of social and political customs. It will not answer all the questions, but it will help you with the surprises and expected hassles. As you search, save interesting articles for future trips. Once you travel, you will start to think of your next trip before you unpack.

The internet offers everything from inexpensive airfares, visa requirements, health warnings, immunization requirements, weather conditions, available restaurants, and hotels. Hotels are easy. You don't have to guess. You know that a western style hotel has a trusted solution for you and a local manager or staff that will help you answer many questions as you need to learn new customs. Internet newsgroups contain current information from people living in areas where you might travel, and they may suggest how to make contact with them when there. You can post questions to the rec.travel groups (e.g. rec.travel.asia). You may get answers to even the most hard-to-answer questions. Many foreign exchange students answer questions posted to the "soc.cultures.country" (e.g., www.soc.cultures.benin). They will exchange information about their own country, and sometimes you might end up with a contact name for when you arrive. Travel newsgroups and travel magazines online also offer valuable reading materials.

Travel forums or chat rooms offer another way to post questions or leave messages. For example, you plan to take a trip to Timbuktu, and you need to build into your calendar the days of travel for the operation of the boat from Mopti to Timbuktu. For the first-time traveler to a Third or Fourth World country, on-line research can provide practical tips about the cities and the people themselves. NOTE: Keep in mind the best advice about information from any online site: reader beware. Web sites, email, and newsgroup postings without identifiable sources may contain true information, rumors, or hearsay. Your hotel website has nuggets to help you, and when you book, consider calling or emailing the manager for additional hints about local tours and events.

### *FRIENDS*

Ask questions of everyone and anyone you meet. Ask friends about appropriate reading material. After remembering the receptionist at the doctor's office telling me she had taken a trip to Mali, I offered to buy her lunch one day, and she answered a whole notepad of questions with enthusiasm. On rare occasions, she had had the chance to share her trip in this way.

Call your local schools. Find foreign exchange students from your country of interest. They like to share information about their country, and they will speak to anyone who will listen, especially if you offer to buy them a cup of coffee! Maybe you could even invite a foreign exchange student to have a meal with you at a local restaurant that serves food from his/her country (your treat, of course). The owner or employees of that restaurant may also help if they call that country "home."

Returning Peace Corps volunteers will have current information about the country they lived in. Call the national headquarters to find out about students returning from your country of interest. Friends and neighbors could possess a wealth of information, good and bad. Your sources may offer conflicting advice, or offer unreliable information, so be sure to ask if the information comes from a recent trip. Out-of-date or second-hand facts need verification. Whenever anyone gives you information about their time in your country of choice, find out where they stayed, what they had to eat, how they spent their days, what they enjoyed or disliked about the country. Be specific when asking questions. Do not depend on advice, as two people with the same travel preferences might have opposite perceptions of the same place.

Also, when speaking to people who have traveled to the country you would also like to see, consider their motivations for having traveled there. Are their motivations the same as yours? After trekking for six hours through deep sand in the Dogon country of Mali, they might expect at least minimum accommodations like a bed, a cool drink, meat and vegetables for dinner. If they had done their research, they would know they would encounter warm Dogon millet beer, or warm boiled water in a tin cup, a bowl of cooked millet, and a flat roof with a woven mat beneath it where they would be forced to sleep under the stars. Then, after waking to the sounds of roosters, their stomachs growling with hunger, these travelers would have listened to the village stirring as the sunlight hit the tops of the cliffs, and would have found themselves unable to go back to sleep. If their idea of a vacation involved a "sleep in", this could very well have been the last straw for them. If your idea of travel is vastly different from theirs, you will not get a clear picture of how much you might enjoy this country, so be sure to ask very pointed questions when interviewing people.

Ask to see friends' photographs and keep an open mind when listening to their tales. We all travel with our own individual views, attitudes, and expectations. The same place may offer a different experience at a different time with changing situations. Do not worry if other people cannot answer all your questions. If they could, you would not need to go anywhere at all to discover for yourself. We all have a different vision of the perfect trip, so we should not believe everything even the expert adventurers tell us about the area. After the trip, you will have your own stories to tell, just as valid as anyone else's about the variegated cultures and the multiplicity of lifestyles you have experienced abroad.

### *MAGAZINES*

Glossy travel magazines may seem like a perfect place to start looking for that ideal adventure location. They appeal to the wealthy tourists looking for tours that do it all for you, except for maybe brushing your teeth. Read magazines like *Transitions Abroad, Passionfruit, Wanderlust, Wend, Asian Geographic, Africa, Afar, Budget Travel, Shermans Travel, Outside, Eco Traveler and National*

*Geographic Adventurer* for ideas on what other adventure travelers have discovered. From the library, check out magazines of conservation organizations like *The Sierra Club, The Nature Conservancy, The National Audubon Society, and National Geographic*. Look at the ads for companies offering free brochures. These can offer ideas on the geography of a place, photographs of the most notable tourist attractions that you might want to avoid, and the in-season perfect [crowded] weather times to cross off your own calendar.

### *NEWSPAPERS*

Newspapers offer travel sections, but most often, they focus on popular tourist sites.

Libraries offer newspapers from the larger cities that feature travel columns and sometimes color photographs. University papers have adventure travel ads and can provide better options than local newspapers, which tend to feature the hottest spots, for example, at the Grand Canyon. Often college and university papers will feature world news and facts.

### *TELEVISION*

Television offers a wealth of programs on travel-related ideas. Many of the educational and public stations show documentaries along with real-life situations in every part of the world imaginable. The travel channel has excellent up-to-date programs on the local level available, from sports in Alaska to cow-jumping in Ethiopia. The cable stations offer movies, filmed in some beautiful and unusual places, which can give substantial background about a place. Look into foreign language films online on sites like Netflix and rent them.

### *LIBRARIES AND OTHER RESOURCES*

Libraries offer travel DVDs, travel guides, and travel narratives that present a full overview of a country. The reference book, "Books in Print," lists thousands of published books by author, subject, or title. A world almanac will give brief facts. Travel narratives, essays, or anthologies may pertain to your potential destination. Do not overlook magazine and newspaper indexes, which help some people to gain an understanding of the perspective of a country and surroundings on paper versus the internet.

Don't overlook the map collection at your local library. Libraries expand the mind by giving us the ability to identify, accumulate, and later recall a variety of information. Open an atlas. Spin the globe, and orient yourself. Photocopying costs little, but remember that enlarging or reducing maps will change the distance scale. Transportation companies like buses, trains, and even airlines, have their own free routing maps. The United States government and some foreign governments have numerous sources with maps. Back road areas will show up on aeronautical maps. Official tourist offices may have maps for the asking. The more detailed the map, the simpler the trip.

A map can serve as your best friend. The regular folding and unfolding and humidity and/or rain can ruin your constant companion, so laminate it, or at least carry it in a Ziploc bag.

### *TOUR OPERATORS*

Tour operators/travel agents offer answers and provide colorful, informative brochures from just about every country you might consider. Agencies share the same interest: they want to convince you of the dangers of travel on your own. They boast of experienced guides who can arrange your attendance at festivals, since they speak the local language. Recommendations include ideas for travel during peak seasons, holidays, or the best weather conditions. Travel operators can often offer advance schedules for transportation and reservations at places to stay.

They want you worrying about the inconveniences you will face if you do not use a travel agent to plan your trip. For example, on your own, you might walk to the river, hoping to catch the next boat to Timbuktu. You might find that because you do not speak the language, it takes you three hours to locate the passenger dock. This would be a problem for many travelers, of course, but for those of us who enjoy adventure travel, it can lead to a delightful and unexpected experience! You might meet some fascinating people while you're searching for your dock, and might, for instance, receive a dinner invitation from the local police officer. The second day you arrive at the correct dock, but the natives inform you through sign language that the boat filled with passengers and the captain decided to leave before the posted time. However, on the way back to your hotel, you meet a Tuareg from the southern edge of the Sahara, who is in town to find a buyer for his salt. He invites you to travel by camel into the desert with his brother and uncle as soon as you reach Timbuktu. The third day you arrive in plenty of time at the dock, board the boat, and drift off dreaming about your next escapade.

With an organized tour, you would have left on the first day and wasted a good part of the day waiting for late arrivals. The tour group might not have offered you the chance for conversation and dinner with a new local friend, or exposed themselves to desert conditions with a Tuareg group by camel.

A tour operator's itinerary plans each day. Pre-organized factory tours often lead to demanding salesmen, wanting to sell their wares or expecting to earn a hefty tip. A boat trip down the Amazon stops at a local village. Before the boat's arrival, the locals change from their western clothing to loincloths, holding spears and hand-carved bows and arrows.

If, on your own, you wish to follow the general route from the calendar of a tour company, allow yourself at least twice the time, or maybe even more. Remember, repetitive tours have arrangements made months in advance. Do not risk disappointment by adding frustration to your trip, trying to see too much in not enough time. Allow plenty of time to experience must-see attractions.

Check www.asta.org, an association of travel professionals and the companies whose products they sell.

### *LANGUAGES*

No language reaches more people in the world than English. We take its advantages for granted. However, you can make a friend if you take the time to try to learn at least a few words in the local language. Your chosen area might require a trip so remote that your local bookstore cannot find a phrasebook with that language. Reserve the time to learn as many important phrases as you can. If you decide to venture into an area too dangerous or remote for anyone other than the adventure traveler, make sure you find a young man for a guide and make sure he speaks at least a little of the language of the villages you'll visit.

### *TOURIST OFFICES*

Tourist offices have a wealth of information available. Most countries have tourist offices in their capital cities. Tourist Boards from most countries exist in the United States, as well as in the countries themselves. Look for National Tourist Boards or a Ministry of Tourism. They all serve the same purpose: promotion of tourism. Some will refer you to travel agents within the country. The best will go all-out and send a complete packet of train schedules, information on where to shop, facts about religious customs, a list of holidays, and ideas on the best sightseeing trips. Save time by making e-mail inquiries to various agencies and boards.

### *ADVENTURE TOUR OPERATORS*

Preplanned expeditions offer opportunities to travel with adventure-tour operators that have solved all the problems and overcome the hassles found along the way. They take care of many of the time-consuming tasks such as researching and sending you a list of what to pack, and when and how to obtain your visa. They will take care of all your equipment needs, such as mosquito nets, rubber boots for jungle treks, and sleeping bags, and they plan the food for every meal. They make up calendars so you can keep track of every minute. They make sure you have permits (necessary in most Third and Fourth World countries when in remote areas) which have the appropriate stamps of approval before you reach a village. I have never had a problem obtaining permits because prior research taught me where to go and what to have available upon arrival. Meeting with local police begins the adventure. They never speak English and what a fun challenge to help them with the information they need on your permit.

Adventure-travel operators can get into countries closed to tourists, but so can anyone else armed with a little confidence and research. You will build strong friendships with tour-mates who have the same desire for excitement in traveling that you have. The experience of adventure traveling is so much richer an experience than your typical European vacation. If you decide to map out your own adventure, find as many travel agency catalogs as you can for a great source of ideas. Your hotel at the destination can be helpful in sharing reports on local guides.

Look for travel agencies with a good reputation and read or listen to reviews from previous clients. Check out www.backroads.com, or www.rei.com/adventure, or www.mtsobek.com, or www.wildernesstravel.com, or www.jul.com (where you get to scuba dive to your hotel room-- located on the ocean floor!

### *GUIDEBOOKS*

Many pros at adventure traveling claim that the key ingredients for a successful trip must include a sturdy pair of hiking boots, a detailed map, and the all-important tool: a good guidebook. The guidebook serves as your authoritative manual, your best friend, your travel agent, your mother, your police officer, and your doctor. Guidebooks have all sorts of information buried inside that will allow you to travel on your own, rather than with a tour group. The best time to study guidebooks? Use them at the very beginning of your research, when you seek ideas. To get familiar with a place, read the beginning chapters on customs, politics, flora, fauna, etc. The next sections on "how-to" will teach you everything you need to know from basic interpretations of language to how to find a toilet.

Libraries offer guidebooks for review on their shelves, and you can also request them through inter-library loans. Do not dwell too much on finding the latest issues for your initial search. The facts and how-to rules do not change much year-to-year.

Guidebooks take many forms. Some dwell on places to visit like the churches or temples with facts from history. Those books provide background information but do not focus on the people and how they live. Look for books that deal with the practical side of life, the ones the adventure traveler needs to read and live by while visiting those countries and those people. A guidebook will prepare you, but it will not pull you along or promise a successful trip. Read and understand the guidebook, and add a healthy dose of adaptability into your own mind and spirit. These two ingredients will protect you like an invisible raincoat worn at all times--even without the rain.

A travel guidebook helps you hike down the path to a global adventure, making it straightforward and less complicated. Budget travelers will find their travel influenced by their choice of guidebooks. Some guidebooks offer details about out-of-the-way and off-the-map places. Budget travelers will want to look for books with alternatives on how to get to those places and where to stay while there.

Travelers on the "pancake trail" (the road traveled by adventure travelers where they find cafes, and bars, all frequented by international budget travelers) will want to search for information that could lead them to a place where other travelers hang out. Travelers can gather ideas at these places and get ideas on events and adventures they might like to seek out that they did not know existed. They can relax, and hang out with other like-minded people while unwinding. No matter how many guidebooks you read, no amount of book-preparation can substitute for the reality of experiencing any situation.

Remember that people write guidebooks! Perfect people do not exist. Opinions, attitudes, choices will vary with every individual and every guidebook.

Look for up-to-date books to take with you. The term "updated" does not necessarily mean re-written or newly researched. The author may not have visited the hotels but instead called to verify any change in services. Businesses change owners and locations. Often, I have found hotels change names or even completely disappear in Third and Fourth World countries, which is another good excuse to visit the current website. The train that the book listed as arriving on Tuesdays at 9:00 a.m. may not even exist by the time you travel there.

Note that different guidebooks offer more details than others. In Sanjiang, China the guidebook suggested taking a bus to the Ma'an Village to see the Wind and Rain Bridge which took the Dong People twelve years to build. The book does not mention that you arrive at the east bus station but need to get to the west station at Ma'an in order to catch the departing bus. When I asked the clerk at the station when the bus left for Ma'an, she shook her head and pointed away. I got my map out and showed her where I wanted to go, and she shook her head and pointed away again. Taxis lined the outside curb, and each driver pointed away. I felt lost and confused and started walking and kept asking people on the sidewalk how to find the bus to Ma'an. Everyone kept pointing away. Did they want me to leave them alone? A few blocks later, trails of buses lined the curb of the west bus station. The first driver I saw pointed to the second bus in line when I asked for a bus to Ma'an. Had I not kept walking and asking, I would never have found the bus leading to Ma'an. When you travel in other countries, be prepared ahead of time, but understand there are some things you cannot be prepared for. Sometimes you will just have to go with the flow!

You can put together your own guidebook, the best by far. First, remember that any book you check out of the library or buy will weigh too much for comfort while traveling. Moreover, you will not need all the information it contains. Instead of bringing a number of heavy books along with you, copy sections of several books pertaining to your trip. From the beginning of your research, keep notes in a spiral notebook, adding information as you find it. Staple together all the pages you've copied from books, and place them in the back of your spiral notebook. Keep your hotel address inside the front cover of your notebook, too, in case you leave it on the seat of your bus one day, and make sure you have pasted in a calendar on the inside front flap of your notebook with a suggested itinerary, followed by places to stay and places to eat. In the back of the notebook, add addresses and phone numbers of emergency contacts and friends and neighbors. You will forget many numbers once you start out on the road. Take your notebook to the bookstore and library with you before you leave on your journey, and pencil in ideas you come up with while researching and dreaming about your trip. When you have it all assembled, you can call this notebook your "journey notebook," your "road book" or "travel diary," whatever suits you. Ask other travelers along the way if you can see their journals. Borrow their ideas if they do not mind.

Your guidebook can serve as your closest friend, one you will get to know quite well before the end of your trip. Consult the appendix in this book for the favorite guidebooks of travelers whom I have met while traveling. If you have an e-book reader, load an e-book guidebook on your reader or laptop to save space and weight.

Remember that expensive electronic gadgets tempt thieves watching for unsuspecting tourists in train and bus stations, and on public transportation wherever the traveler may find it. Not only may you lose your expensive iPad to thieves while traveling, you may also find that you don't have electricity to power it up at the moment you need a map. So leave the iPad home or take it with you and guard it carefully, but never leave your only map on it! See section above on Libraries, specifically the section on maps and map care.

### CLIMATE

Once you have chosen your destination (or perhaps a general direction for travel), you might have the option of considering when to leave on your adventure. Business schedules, college vacation time, or holiday periods may dictate your time for travel. Avoid the peak season. Every country has peak travel times, even a country not well traveled. Wealthier families spend their holiday or vacation time during the best weather periods at some of the same spots you might visit. This does not mean you have to time your trip during the rainy season. However, if you go at the beginning or end of the peak season, you will avoid the crowds and the higher prices. The rainy season in some countries means a light afternoon shower, which cools the temperature without bothering your travels in any way. If you plan a multi-stop trip, decide the most important places to see in favorable weather. Plan your trip with that stop occurring during good weather. Sometimes, the price of airfare will determine when you go on your trip. Peak season airline prices can kill your budget.

Climate could vary with latitude and altitude within a country. Even in a small country like Chile, you can climb a glacier in a down jacket and boots one day, and the next day, wearing shorts and sunscreen, you can gather shells on a beach. Also, remember that time zones might shorten or lengthen days after you leave home, and hours of business change from country to country.

Words can have different meanings from culture to culture. The word "holiday" means vacation in many countries. If planning to see festivals and dancing in a small town, you might arrive to find the town's businesses closed due to a holiday. Once, in the Swiss Alps, I had traveled all night by train to visit a small village during their holiday. After the train left me standing alone with my four-year-old daughter Carrie, I wondered why we saw no people about. A horse pulling a sleigh came by. The driver spoke no English but realized we needed a place to stay. He took us to the one hotel in town, closed for the "holiday." He found a key, and a woman down the block came in and showed us a room, how to turn the lights on, how to operate the toilet and bath. She walked us to the kitchen, opened the cupboards, smiled, and left. For several days, the two of us stayed alone in this great hotel with twelve-inch thick feather beds as we visited the town and small villages in the mountain by sleigh. Would you ever think that a holiday in America would actually close a hotel? Do your research, and be prepared!

Of course, you can never plan perfect weather, so let your budget and your calendar dictate when you travel. However, research will help in preparing for even the unsuspected surprise.

### *LENGTH OF STAY*

How to judge the length of time it will take to accomplish visiting an area depends on all the unknowns in the puzzle. Many travelers will try to fit as many pieces of a country into one trip as they can, and sometimes plan for several countries, since they came so far. They may think, "I might not come back to this area, so why not do and see as much as I'm able." This attitude will cause you to overbook your calendar because you can't judge how long it will take to arrive at your destination, proceed with what you had planned, and move on to the next place.

Expect delays in Third and Fourth World countries. According to the *Lonely Planet Mali* guidebook, the flights out of Mopti, in the country of Mali, West Africa, operated three days a week at 1:00PM. It took hours in the airport for me to find someone who knew about the flight schedules. The ticket agent I found to help me, announced that the planes flew only on Friday that week, and I had arrived on Monday! My whole itinerary changed in a flash, since I now lost a whole week. I wanted to spend that week in Timbuktu, not Mopti.

A big factor in influencing how long your trip will last involves your budget. Using guidebooks and other research (ideas from friends or acquaintances who traveled there, stories you read in magazines, and travel narratives from bookstores or the library), estimate how much money you will spend preparing for and taking your trip. See the Appendix for ideas on which guidebooks give useful information on costs.

Take into consideration how you want to pace yourself when you are determining how long things will take. This will help you estimate your length of stay. Do you want to settle in and have a meaningful relationship with locals to remember, or would you prefer to get to as many places as possible just to say you were there? The museums, galleries, temples, or ruins viewed on the travel channel and in glossy travel magazines tempt us. However, for me, wandering through a market and interacting with the locals, is much more rewarding. I ingest and absorb more about a culture in interaction with its people than in viewing the typical sights referenced in books.

You need time and patience to sense the rhythm of a village. You can't rush this experience. Meandering the hidden paths of a small village in Borneo, I noticed several women carrying babies in elaborate beaded baby carriers, all entering the same building. The makeshift building with its tin roof piqued my curiosity. Oversized foreign words hung sideways outside the window on a swinging sign. Inside I discovered two people in white coats giving injections to children. I managed to figure out that the doctors came once a month to these jungle villages to check on the health of children. The mothers showed off their children and the detail work on the baby carriers their ancestors had stitched. These carriers were then passed down through generations of women. Do not visit a place and leave so soon that you wonder if you ever arrived. The importance of the journey depends on what you bring back with you.

### *GETTING AWAY FOR A WEEK OR TWO*

Conservative plans work best when you are writing your itinerary. Try to plan so you do not rush through each day to reach every intended excursion. Allow twice as much time for travel and finding all those little out-of-the-way places to eat and sleep. I try to plan half my trip with details of where and what I want to see. I allow a few days in-between for discovery. A rendezvous with spontaneous and serendipitous encounters may happen on these days.

Take a week to go to one place in one country, spend time seeing the sights, and then allow a few days for interaction with the people. Avoid constructing strict calendars with every minute planned; this will save you frustration. Why, you ask, would you be frustrated by a rigid traveling agenda? Because you will find things happen differently than planned in a foreign country, and you'll want to leave some of your trip to chance.

To make a short trip more memorable, do something out of the ordinary. Take a bicycle trip around Lake Atitlan in Guatemala and feast on the colorful sights along the way, or, in Ecuador, take a river journey into the Amazon, stay in jungle villages and sleep under mosquito nets. Peru could work for beginning adventurers. After climbing among the ruins of Machu Picchu, take a train to Puno, and then a boat to the Floating Islands to revel in the life of the Uros people. They live on islands made of reeds. The men fish for a living in boats made of the same reeds. You may chance upon some extraordinary and unexpected surprises that will enrich you with a deeper understanding of Peru than if you had stayed in Lima and visited monuments and museums.

Perhaps you would like to get away for two weeks. If so, you might pick one country and pinpoint the principal sights to see in that country. For example, you could spend two memorable weeks in Bangkok. The hustle-bustle of downtown (including beautiful temples on the river and fascinating monasteries), would fill your desire for the educational and photographic experience. I never sensed closeness to the people while traveling in Bangkok; unfortunately, I remained a foreigner. However, I did spend a week up north and visited factories as well as candy and jewelry makers, all willing to share their craft-making abilities with me. A trek into the northern jungles gave me the opportunity to meet the Karen tribe, a welcoming group of people whose wide open doors into their lives taught me a lot about contentment.

Reduce the stress of your departure by implementing advanced planning. Give yourself many months to prepare and modify your attitudes. Start note taking and record any thoughts that come to mind (like canceling your newspaper and remembering to have the post office hold your mail). Allow plenty of time for your actual departure. Pack days in advance to allow time for the unexpected.

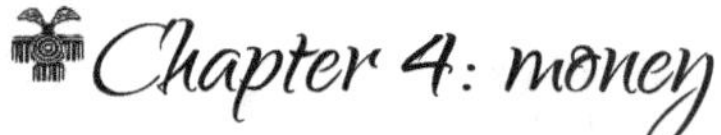

*"I travel not to go anywhere, but to go. I travel for travel's sake. The great affair is to move."* Robert Louis Stevenson

***WHAT CAN YOU AFFORD?***

The amount of money you need for your travels will depend on destination and living requirements. Research the cost of living in the country you plan to visit. Spend time on the internet researching or talking with those just returning in forums offered online (like "Thorn Tree" or "Lonely Planet") for ideas on the costs you will incur for your area of travel. Do not assume that a small, remote village, island, or country costs less than downtown Bangkok.

For instance, traveling to the lip-disc-wearing Mursi tribe (hidden from all tourist itineraries, deep in the jungles of Ethiopia) will cost you a fortune. Travel agents expose wealthy tourists to the unusual habits of the Mursi. Those tourists, unaware of their impact, leave huge tips to tribes-people posing for cameras. As a result, the aggressive tribe expects hefty tips from all visitors.

Many parts of Asia and South and Central America cost little for even a two-week trip. Realize that the more time you spend in a country, the more you will find cheaper ways of doing things. To figure your base budget, start by deciding what kind of shelter you prefer, your food requirements, whether you want to try local foods (or eat like a king at the favorite tourist restaurants), and include local travel costs. Add a generous cushion for the unexpected, like several hundred dollars for a two-week trip and $1000 for a month-long trip. You never know when that cash will come in handy. Take into consideration your personal habits; ask yourself, "What must I sacrifice to make this trip happen?" You may decide to give up eating out and expensive entertainment here at home so you can save up enough money to stay on the beach during your overseas trip. Determine your priorities. Then be sure to add in extra cash in case you need a change of pace even if it is just for one night.

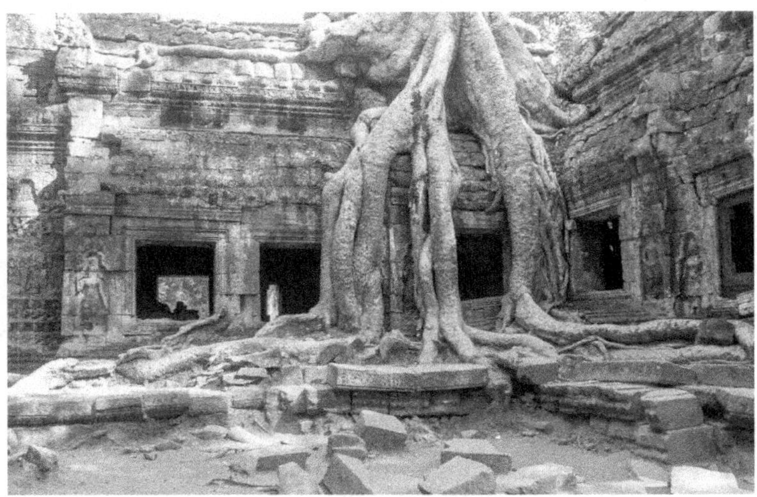

*5. Angkor Wat, Cambodia*

Traveling by bus while in other countries, versus using a plane, can reduce the costs of travel. Guidebooks will list prices for hotels and restaurants, but watch out for out-of-date guidebooks. Add 10% or more for inflation to everything. To save money on food, eat at sit-down restaurants as little as possible. The corner *tiendas* (tiny grocery stores), street vendors, open markets, and pastry shops populate the smallest of towns.

Even if you travel within the United States, Europe, or Japan, by watching your budget, you can save cash, provided you do not insist on traveling in luxury. Not shopping around for the best airfares and traveling by taxis will soon deplete your spending money.

Traveling with a lot of money insulates us from the reality of our world. We tend to fall back into the familiar when we carry cash. We eat, sleep, and go to the expected tourist traps and don't get out there and see the real world. I have to admit, after a month of eating power bars and foil-packed tuna without bread (no bread in rural China), I had to give in to the MacDonald's at the train station in Changsha on the return to Hong Kong. My excitement in thinking about real biscuits and gravy with scrambled eggs and pancakes kept me awake all night.

My disappointment with their limited with no breakfast choices caused me to find the nearest comfortable hotel, knowing their buffet would fill me until I returned home.

Visiting the poorer countries of the world, those where most of the world's population earns less than $2 a day, will also protect your budget. In these places, you will find it easy to meet beautiful people and see incredible sights without spending a lot of cash. Encountering the everyday lives of these people will build your memories and awaken your senses too!

People in Third and Fourth World countries live the definition of contentment, despite the desire for possessions we find essential by our standards. Their wealth lies, not in materialism, but in the human spirit.

Rather than pity their situation by comparing their mode of living to your standards, open yourself to capturing the spirit of their wealth, their values. When sought, their riches will reward you. These people, content with what little they have, teach reality lessons to the world. Considering the exchange rates of different countries might help you to decide where to travel. Research in guidebooks and on the Internet will give you ideas of exchange rates. In addition, larger banks have information about the exchange rates of common international destinations.

If Ecuador offers an attractive rate on the dollar, that might influence your decision to travel there. If the US dollar starts losing value against that nation's currency, things will cost more there than you expected. However, if the dollar gains, you will go home with more money (or have more to spend when there). Remember though, the exchange rates might suddenly change, not necessarily in your favor. Prepare for the dollar to decline by bringing extra cash when you travel.

Unexpected setbacks cost time and money in First and Second World Countries. Learning by doing in more economical countries, you have room for mistakes by spending less money in the beginning. Remember, foreign money looks like monopoly money.

Several thousand units of their currency can represent coins in US currency. If cashing a hundred dollars in India today, you would get over a million rupiah, which expands not only your feeling of wealth but your wallet as well. Spend with wisdom and understanding. Traveling on the cheap develops your ingenuity. Get help from locals and live as they do. The money you save by low-cost traveling will enable you to have more travel time, but will also allow you to develop valuable interactions with the people, thus building memories to take back with you.

***BEFORE YOU GO***

You will spend a great deal of money before you go on your trip, including your largest expense, the airline tickets. Passport and visa costs vary around the world. The internet gives the most current information. A visa to Bolivia or China today would cost over $100. If time and the opportunity exist, arrange for visas in the foreign country at the airport or the stop before arriving at the final destination. For example, a layover in Bangkok for two days saves money and time if you use it to obtain a visa for Laos or Myanmar. Check the internet and guidebooks to see if the country requires you to have a visa before arriving or if you may obtain one at the airport when entering that country.

Handling and overnight mail costs add up, also. In requesting a visa from home, I allow myself a couple of months or more for visa processing. During a phone conversation with the Consular or Embassy of your destination, ask many questions and make sure you are filling out all the forms they need. Otherwise, you might end up with your passport returned for resubmission a few more times due to lack of information.

When I tried to get a visa for Ethiopia, I had to send in my passport four times with different information each time. The embassy or consular office would list the requirements on the phone, sometimes forgetting to ask me for something they needed, or asking me for the wrong amount of money.

Luggage, although a great investment, remains another upfront cost. A good soft-sided travel pack (4000-6000 cubic inches), whether it has wheels and/or converts to a backpack, can cost several hundred dollars. Buy luggage that fits your needs. You will live out of it for several weeks. Does it need to be expensive? No. Does it need to be quality? Yes. Do not expect to replace it along the way if the straps break or the zipper sticks. On one trip, my bag would not zip. I packed everything of value in small plastic rice sacks as a carry-on and stuffed all the rest in a huge rice sack (durable plastic sacks used for shipping rice). My favorite type of travel bag is a soft-sided canvass type bag with wheels. It expands for new purchases and is lighter weight than a standard rectangular carry-on.

Deciding on new clothing for a trip depends on your mode of travel (see chapter on packing).

Travel clothing differs from your normal street clothes, so plan to invest in attire such as rain gear, suited for your destination. Good quality (and comfortable) shoes or hiking boots will ensure comfort for any trip. Buy what suits your style of travel and break footwear in at least a month before travel.

Immunizations and medical supplies can cost a couple of hundred dollars. You will need a few immunizations in Third and Fourth World countries but make the investment and play it safe (see chapter on immunizations). A private doctor will charge well over $100. If you get six shots, they start to add up fast. If your polio and tetanus boosters need updating, add that cost. Stocking a first aid kit, buying a second pair of glasses, filling prescriptions, acquiring antibiotics for emergencies, and getting that long-needed physical should rank high on your list of things to get out of the way early on. For most tropical trips, you will need Malarone. (Check online for the latest malaria preventive medication).

You will need to plan for the other miscellaneous items required for the area you have chosen. You will want to think about camping supplies, a new sleeping bag, a durable tent made for your form of travel, and water filters to name just a few items A trip to Ethiopia required my sleeping out in the open in the jungle and desert areas. To save money, I expended considerable research on shopping for lightweight gear that could endure the extremes of this trip.

After much effort, I found a basic one-man tent, weighing less than three pounds, for under a $100. Not until I slept in three inches of water one night did I regret not buying a more expensive, waterproof tent. I used the spray waterproofing on all the seams, but they gave way to water anyway. Avoid making the same mistake I made; buy quality, and spend the extra money so you can enjoy your trip.

Other items, like those extra memory cards for digital cameras, can be purchased more cheaply online than in the local stores. Do not forget the cost of processing when you return if you use film cameras.

### *HIDDEN MONEY*

The most important information I can provide to you about traveling concerns keeping your valuables safe. Money, passport, and credit cards belong in a money belt, close to your body, and under your clothing. A money belt made of soft cotton or nylon with a waist belt or thin rope can hang around your neck.

Remind yourself that your money belt serves as your lifeline while traveling. Keep everything in a Ziploc bag inside the money belt to protect it from sweat.

Do not let other people see your money or watch you counting it. In a Third or Fourth World country, the money you carry might amount to more than a local would make in a year. Do not take more money than you will need, or you may risk losing the extra money. If you fear not having enough money, take credit cards to access cash.

When traveling in a poor country, consider hiding your money and documents in several places. You can wear a neck pouch for everyday spending money and keep documents, airline tickets, and most of your cash in your waist money belt under your clothes. Hiding a little money in your backpack helps you recover in case you have a loss or robbery while out shopping, and your bags remain at the hotel.

Use your imagination for hiding money. While traveling in remote parts of Burma, I divided my money and hid it in different places like in my shoes. I put a few hundred-dollar bills inside a prescription pill bottle leaving a few pills in the bottle so if someone picked it up, it would sound like a normal pill bottle. When my daughter Katherine and I were traveling in the Amazon, I heard a horror story from a couple traveling with us. Thieves forced all the foreigners off their bus and stripped them to their underwear. They went through their luggage, taking money and passports. The woman kept her bra on and that is where she had hidden some of their money. On subsequent travel trips, my shirt size increased. I cut the cups from a bra and sewed them inside an identical bra, leaving the tops of the inserted cups unsewn. This gave me a space to hide money.

### *CASH*

Determining how much cash to carry requires your careful attention. Destination and activities dictate the amount. If you stay in a city with a bank that cashes traveler's checks or has an ATM, you need to have enough cash with you for a couple of days or so and plan on cashing traveler's checks or using the debit/credit card when you must. If you visit a smaller city bank, they will exchange US dollars ONLY if they look new. In Third or Fourth World countries, they may not take torn or worn bills of any denomination even if you plead. Banks and hotels prefer hundred dollar bills. Also, do not accept worn bills of the local currency because you cannot exchange or spend them anywhere.

Small denominations and local notes have more uses than larger ones, so use the smaller notes when necessary to pay for cheap bus rides and snacks, etc. If in a retail store, restaurant or hotel, you should pay with larger bills. Do not expect a seller in a local market to have change for a large denomination bill.

Sometimes in your hometown, you can buy foreign currency, which may include an excessive service charge. Call larger banks and ask if they can obtain the currency for you. You do not have to procure foreign money ahead of time, though. When traveling abroad, you can bring your own currency from home and exchange it at the airport or withdraw local currency from a local ATM when you reach the foreign country. If you arrive after hours or cannot find local currency, have several one-dollar bills to use for a taxi to your hotel until you find local money. Large airports offer currency exchange booths that are open all night. In your research try to find data on costs you will have along the way. Unknown opportunities hide around every corner. Allow for spontaneous changes in your plans.

### *TRAVELER'S CHECKS*

Traveler's checks still exist in today's modern society of automation with plastic cards. The safety a traveler feels from not carrying huge amounts of cash does not come free. Most banks charge a fee for cashing traveler's checks.

Some countries will accept only certain bank checks, so do some research and check with your guidebook. Every bank that cashes traveler's checks has cashed American Express for me, but do not depend on that. Some banks will not cash any, and some will cash only certain denominations, so carry a variety of denominations. In some countries, counterfeit money causes problems so ask whether businesses take all denominations of money. In Timbuktu (Mali), not one person would take the fifty CFA bill I tried to spend even though it looked clean. In the same country of Mali, the city of Djenne would not take any twenty CFA bills. Without a bank in town and carrying only traveler's checks and twenty CFA bills, I told my hotel I had no choice.

The hotel and the bus company finally did take the twenties, but it was a big hassle. They explained that in some parts of the country, thieves pass counterfeit twenties, and the police alert the businesses to be aware of them.

Write down the serial numbers of your checks and store the list in another location away from your checks. Before your trip, leave a copy of the serial numbers with someone you can call or email to yourself in case you lose everything and must call American Express for money. Traveler's checks should never leave your body until cashed. Insured checks do not eliminate the inconvenience of making a claim for replacement of stolen or lost checks. If you do not have the numbers of the lost checks, you will have to telephone your bank where you purchased them or your friend at home to obtain the list of numbers.

Ask around before paying the one percent fee for the checks. A regular bank customer may have an account that allows for no service fees for traveler's checks.

### *ATMs*

Automated Teller Machines (ATMs) are available in transportation terminals, inside retail stores, and along streets in various towns. These machines are enclosed for your privacy.

The conveniences of the ATM include the absence of long lines, forms to sign and getting local cash after bank hours. When you run out of cash and the ATM network closes or keeps your card, you need to have alternative plans in mind like using another card at the machine across town. Keep in mind the machine may not read your pin number due to some machine failure.

Be prepared to read the options in the foreign language of your location. If you want to cash two hundred dollars in your own currency, you need to put that amount in the local currency when the machine asks how much to cash. Otherwise you will end up with two hundred pesos for example which is less than twenty dollars.

### *PERSONAL CHECKS*

With a few exceptions, you cannot cash regular personal checks abroad. Some foreign banks cash personal checks if you open an account with them. You may be able to cash personal checks at American Express if you have one of their credit cards. International banks offer international bank accounts. Check with your bank for the names of these financial institutions.

### *BARGAINING*

For many, part of the fun of traveling abroad includes bargaining for the crafts, hotels, food, and transportation offered by local tradespeople. If you are the type of person who enjoys this kind of give-and-take, you will find traveling in Third and Fourth World countries very exciting. In these countries, the asking price on any item has nothing to do with the final price you'll pay. Often vendors expect negotiation, so bargain whenever possible. No matter what, the sellers won't come down in price if they see any excitement over the item from the buyer. It helps to have other travelers around you, openly telling you not to buy, to walk away and that the price is too high. This makes the seller nervous about the potential of you walking away, which causes a reaction to make a deal he may not have considered before. Most tourists will never try and bargain at all. The seller knows those odds and may be willing to sell lower than his profit margin just to make a sale. You may run into someone who will not budge on his or her asking price. I always start my bargaining at forty to fifty percent of the asking price with the hopes of paying close to that price. The mind of the one buying determines the value of the product.

Some vendors have dramatic and even outlandish lines rehearsed. When engaged in difficult negotiations with young street vendors, sometimes you just have to walk away. Vendors can use strong language without backing off their initial price. Avoid hassles unless the item that catches your attention is worth the asking price. Almost always the seller will ask for one more price if you give them only one price and stick with it. Offer a few dollars more and then just keep saying, "It's too much, and I don't need it." In most cases the seller will give in as you walk away, and often I get a few feet away before I hear them say, "Okay, okay."

Young entrepreneurs know where to find travelers. You will never have to search for souvenir hawkers, hanging out around bus and train depots, restaurants, and hotels. You have made a substantial financial commitment for this trip, so before bargaining on an item, look around for similar merchandise being sold by other vendors. A woman offered me a pair of rayon pants in a Balinese market for 50,000 rupiah; I thought I could start at half price until I searched a few more booths where the same pants were on sale. One vendor wanted 280,000 rupiah (or twenty-eight dollars) for an identical pair of pants. Several other sellers asked close to 280,000 rupiah, too, so I found my way back to the first vendor and offered her 40,000 for the pants. She accepted, and I happily stashed them in my bag.

Traveling in low season justifies your asking for a lower room rate. Ask for a smaller room, a room without a window, a room on the street side or a higher floor. Food establishments with set prices will not bargain.

When converting currency, language can present problems. Memorize the conversion of one dollar, five dollars, and ten dollars to have a starting point in mind. In remote areas, the individual you encounter may misunderstand your interpretation of how much you expect to pay in his currency. In that case, fingers work well, but sometimes the added zeroes are misunderstood.

In a border-town market, a group of Somalians sold slabs of salt. I wanted to buy the wood bell worn on their camel's neck. I kept pointing to the bell and then to myself. I made motions of taking the bell off the camel, and then I pointed away. The leader of the group of women held up five fingers, meaning five dollars, I thought. Fatigued from the bickering in trying to get a deal, I nodded, and the clan surrounded me. The girl's father, I assumed, pointed his finger at me and with a deep voice shouted a few words. I thought surely, I had offended this tribe and feared what would happen next. The whole group started laughing and shook my hand. The leader of the group untied the bell, and I gave him the money he asked for, I thought. Later that night, a Catholic missionary invited me to his mission for dinner. He had heard the story of a white girl who had some trouble at the market that day. I told him about the confusion over the bell, and he replied that the leader of the group had asked me to give him fifty cents for the bell, and I had given him five dollars! This is more money than these sellers might see in a year as they trade for all their goods. He said that I had made them supremely happy. My interaction with that Berber group continues to be one of my fondest memories of Ethiopia.

Ask the price first before you buy anything or get into a taxi. Agree on a price before reaching for your wallet and try to offer the exact change. Do not start buying handmade baskets at a fair price, only to find out later in the day that a famous village wood carver has some incredible carvings for sale, but you must decline because you have run out of room in your bag.

Remember, "Shop around first and then make your purchases." You cannot spend a lot of time comparing prices and shopping around when you are only in a country for a short time or when you have planned too much into too few days. This is another reason why longer trips can be much more enjoyable for you.

Once while in Ecuador, I rode on the roof of a train. When the train stopped to allow another train to pass, a young boy jumped down and ran into a sugar cane field, grabbing several sticks of cane. Climbing back on the roof, he named his price, and he would not negotiate. He knew he had a sale. Never having tasted sugar cane, I saw this as an opportunity, and he saw this in my eyes. This eleven-year-old orphan rode trains to beg for food and wanted us to adopt him. Begging from tourists, he learned acceptable English and taught us a lot about Ecuador from the roof of that train. Unexpected friendships and information about local events can evolve from the simple act of buying something.

Play the game and walk away if you cannot get your price. If a merchant has a rare item, or he has had a profitable day of business, he might not reduce his asking price. If you have the time, wait until the end of the day to bargain for items; that is when sellers realize the day might end without a sale.

A shop owner in Mali offered me an old horsehair wand, the handle carved of ivory with intricate designs. He asked $100. I knew I could afford ten dollars, apologized for my low offer, and the rest of the day, I snooped about the extraordinary market, never finding anything comparable to a wand that had so many stories to tell. Twice during the day, I asked if he could lower his price, and he did but not enough. Five minutes before his shop closed, I found myself in front of his shop, too embarrassed to go in.

A young girl came running toward me with the wand and wanted the ten dollars. I looked at the shop and the old man grinned and waved as I handed her the money. A skilled negotiator must have confidence and practice. Negotiating will save you money and give you the respect of many locals.

### *NITTY GRITTY*

Research can save you money. Know what other travelers paid for items by asking them after watching their interaction and pay close attention to what bills they use to pay for the purchase. Ask them if they have found that dollars or local currency buys more. Before entering into a bargaining situation, ask yourself about your top dollar for the item so that you have a suitable stopping point.

Bargaining includes any deal you can muster. Buy two for the price of one or if the vendor will not come down on a price, ask him to throw in another item you want. In Ethiopia, I found a six-inch tall stool, covered in beads, on which men rest their heads at night in order to protect their hair-dos. I had seen many men using the stools while resting in the afternoon and wanted this particular style, given to men at their weddings. The owner would not budge on the price. Back and forth we went, making offers and counter-offers. He would wave his hands in the air and yell something, and I would come back with another offer.

While we were negotiating, I noticed a leather basket used to carry injera (the local bread eaten at every meal). Dyed red, it brought back memories from a few days earlier when I watched a woman making the red dye in a tiny village. Without acting excited about the basket, I asked the man to throw the basket in with the stool, and then I would accept his offer. He smiled and handed me the stool and the basket. We laughed and shook hands, and then he invited me to his sister's house for dinner!

Do not begin bargaining unless you intend to buy the merchandise for the final negotiated price. If the seller meets your price, you buy.

Upsetting one merchant by going back on a legitimate sale can give you a bad reputation in the village, and other vendors will hesitate to bargain with you.

In Timbuktu, the bargaining practices range from ferocious haggling to following the potential buyer everywhere. The sellers want to sell you everything or anything before you ask. If you mention a price, you must continue to deal and then complete the buy if the seller gives in to your price.

### *RECORD KEEPING*

Some countries require you to declare how much money you bring into the country and proof when you leave of how much you spent. You will need receipts for every purchase made even if you cannot read the language. Take notepaper, write down the item and price paid, and have a signature of the seller attached. I have run into this problem of needing all receipts for purchased goods twice, both times in Africa. Keep records of which traveler's checks you have used. If you keep complete records, you will avoid unnecessary duties when returning through customs.

### *CREDIT CARDS*

Plastic can help on a trip. If you have a scanner at home, scan your cards and email yourself a copy of the front and back of your card in case you lose it while abroad. Note, though, that scanners in public places are not secure. If you hand your card to a clerk at the drugstore, for instance, and ask her to scan your card front and back, your information will go into their system. Any employee curious enough can go looking for the card info later. Use a scanner at home or ask a trusted friend to scan your card. Many foreign airlines and tour companies will ask to see the credit card you used to secure the reservation. This happened to me when I flew with China Airlines. Because I did not have with me the credit card I had used to make the reservation, I had to use another credit card for identification. Keep records of your expenditures or you may go into shock when your bill arrives at home. It can take about two months to receive all your bills from a foreign country. Depending on your spending habits, you might want to place a credit limit on your card while you travel. You might limit your use of the card to emergencies and expensive purchases. If you have the money and want to splurge on entertainment and shopping, then increase the limit.

Do not lose sight of your card when using it. In an overseas shop, a merchant took my card to the back by the imprinting machine. He made two receipts: one was phony on which he charged several hundred dollars' worth of merchandise.

Back home, I could not fight the bill as I did not know the name of the shop, and it had no phone or address anyway. Keep track of your customer copy and make sure the business name and phone number appear on the copy so that you can compare it with your bill. Exchange rates will differ when using credit cards.

Ask what rate the merchant uses and if they add a charge for credit card use. Unlike retail stores in the United States that absorb the additional charges for card use, foreign stores attach that charge to the buyer.

Make sure the seller writes the sales draft in the currency of the local country on the draft, for example, FR400 (meaning you bought the items in France for 400 francs). Credit cards charge service fees and a percentage of the total received, but stiff competition has many card companies eliminating those service fees. Check how your credit card company handles these issues before you leave this country.

Some ATM machines will only accept a four-digit pin, so change your code if more than four numbers. Cards often have twenty-four hour maximum limits.

Use caution when using your pin on your credit, or any cards, as thieves watch ATM machines and phone booths with binoculars for pin numbers. Use caution when leaving an ATM and use them only during daylight hours. Thieves watch where you put your money. Use waist belts under your clothing and wear your cash. Reduce total transaction costs by withdrawing larger amounts of cash. Let your bank know about your upcoming travel plans before you leave. Your bank or credit card company will place a block on your account if your transaction pattern changes. That includes all domestic travel to other states as well as foreign. Some foreign banks and ATMs only accept cards with computer chips in them. Check your own company to see if that is available and if they have special cards for traveling without overseas transaction fees.

### *BUDGETING*

Before you go, you will need to determine a budget. Estimate how much each day will cost, including international airfare, internal air, bus or train transportation, shelter, food, shopping and fun. The best way to begin a budget plan is through research. For example, go to the library and open any *Lonely Planet* guidebook.

Open to any chapter about an area and find the list of hotels. Look for places to eat, things to do, and directions, etc. By adding about fifteen percent to the guidebook figures, a traveler can figure a budget for the entire trip.

Stay within your budget while you travel to prevent running out of money. If you spend more money one day, then try not to overspend the next couple of days.

Making a little chart in your notebook also works. No need to buy a fancy calculator that converts money into different currencies. With a little practice, a traveler can figure out the conversion rate rather quickly. Think about all the hidden costs involved in traveling. The list includes airport parking, taxis, overweight luggage fees, tips, and porters. Hotels and restaurants charge up to twenty percent for their services. Also, think about items not included in your tour like extra meals, beverages, souvenirs, and room service.

### *BARTERING*

Trading goods or services works well as a universal method of exchange. Anything a traveler carries could have value when traveling in remote areas.

Did you bring too many clothes? You can use that to your advantage by trading clothes with a service provider for something you want. For instance, often a guide will work off part of his wages for gear or clothing.

In the Amazon, my guide Luis did not have the opportunity to buy a tent, but I could replace my own without much trouble when I returned to the United States.

For part of my payment to Luis, I traded my tent at the end of the trip. Another example of trading involved the rubber boots I bought from Luis. He had spent four dollars on them, and I bought them from him for that same amount. I fell in love with them! Many a tarantula crossed over them during my jungle walks and vice-versa, and they were well worth four dollars to me. Tee shirts and socks also make for easy trades. The difficult part of trading involves valuing the item. In Third and Fourth World countries, people will ask for your hiking boots quite often. The boots may equal the worth of what that individual earns in an entire year. Rare, handcrafted items passed down through the centuries could match the value of your shoes and the shirt off your back. You can best determine the value of the trade.

***BLACK MARKET***

Locals on the street will offer to exchange your money for a higher exchange rate than the bank will offer. To entice you to buy through the black market, they will tell you anything. They will tell you the banks just closed. They will say you need to trade your money to get the local currency, or that the banks will not accept US dollars or traveler's checks. The black market flourishes as an ILLEGAL way to transfer money. Some countries prosecute those who trade in the black market.

***RUN OUT OF MONEY?***

You can obtain cash abroad with most credit cards. ATM machines appear in major cities but not in remote areas.

They have a dollar limit per day and the rate of exchange on the day the bill clears in the US determines the amount, not the rate in effect on the day of your transaction. You will receive the local currency, not dollars, when using an ATM. Try to avoid the expensive and time-consuming process of having money wired to you.

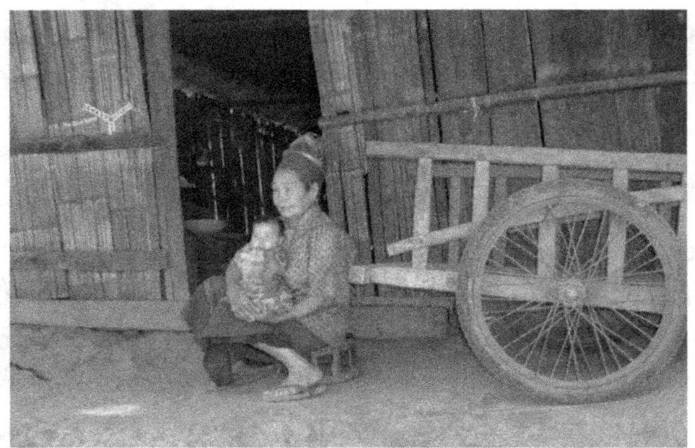

*6. Woman with grandchild, remote village, Cambodia*

### *BECOME FAMILIAR WITH LOCAL CURRENCY*

Think in terms of the local currency. Know the coins and bills. When bargaining, you will not have time to stop and calculate the equivalents in US dollars. A working knowledge of the country's currency will help you adjust to the country's economy. Holding ten thousand rupiah in your hand takes some getting used to after you accept the idea that it is really worth one American dollar. Make a small chart of conversions and keep handy in a back pocket until you get used to dealing in local currency.

### *EMERGENCY STASH*

Keep some money back home instead of spending every penny on your vacation. A cash reserve will get you by when you return home, so you do not have the worry of how to survive while you go through the culture shock of your return. If you run out of money or need medical help requiring cash, you will have an emergency backup.

### *TRAVEL FOR FREE*

Use your imagination. There are many creative ways to get all, or part, of your travel free:

1. Rent out your house while you are away, or do a home exchange with people in the country where you are heading. Some advantages of staying in someone's home include free local phone service, internet, and a kitchen. A local resident will share favorite places for food and special sites, not listed in your guidebook.

2. Check out online forums and boards for house sitting. Sometimes you might find a place to stay in exchange for watering plants or caring for someone's pets. Look for homes in college and church communities. Also, check social media like Facebook and Craigslist. In addition, it would be helpful to check www.housesittersAmerica.com or www.housecarers.com. For San Miguel de Allende, Mexico read the Civil List forum and find people wanting pet and house sitters for various time periods.

3. Deliver a car to Florida. Have your transportation and gas paid for while you see the country. Relocation and rental car companies need cars delivered quickly due to seasonal demands. Advertise in community and college newspapers. Look in cities you want to travel to as well as the city where you live.

4. If you are a boat captain, deliver a boat to the Caribbean.

5. Crewing a yacht earns working passage. If you are mechanically inclined or have navigational skills, you could earn a paycheck. Check www.crewseekers.net, bulletin boards in port towns and ask boat captains if they could use another crewmember.

6. Sleeping in a convent or monastery can save you money as more and more of these places are beginning to offer rooms for rent to help pay for the aging structures. Although they might not offer to change your bed linens, nuns and monks open their century-old homes, allowing the traveler to escape the hustle and bustle of hotels and to experience a hospitality tradition that has been around for 1500+ years. Check one or both sites: www.monasterystays.com, or www.goodnightandgodbless.com/accomodation.html

7. Find a timeshare in an area you are interested in staying a night or two. By listening to a ninety-minute talk about the timeshare, you will earn free nights and other options like discount tickets to theme parks or coupons for meals.

8. Give a lecture on a cruise ship or at a conference and have some enquire whether you may have your travel expenses covered. Check www.cruiselinesjobs.com or www.jobships.com.

9. Volunteer for some organizations that pay for room and board.

10. In remote areas, barter your labor at a hostel for a free room. Trading labor for room and board is a way to get around the problems with working visas in foreign countries. Look for job postings online on sites such as www.hostelworld.com listed on their message board.

### ***RETURNING HOME***

Change all your foreign currency into US dollars before your return to the United States. Local banks will charge outrageous fees to convert your foreign currency. Some foreign bills like CFAs from Ethiopia will not convert to dollars.

# Chapter 5: health and insurance

*"The use of traveling is to regulate imagination by reality, and instead of thinking how things may be, to see them as they are."* Samuel Johnson

## *PREPARATIONS*

The Center for Disease Control and the International Traveler's Hotline have information available by phone, Internet, fax and mail. www.cdc.gov. They offer current US government requirements for immunizations and anti-malarial recommendations. Health clinics or doctors specializing in travel health will have this information. The CDC also lists the health hazards of each region in the world, ideas for disease prevention, and current outbreaks of disease or epidemics. The CDC recommends immunizations that do not appear as requirements by governments of other countries. Use your best judgment, regarding immunizations.

After deciding where to travel, contact the International Association for Medical Assistance to Travelers (IAMAT). Several months before traveling, write for their package and a membership card or copy their info from online. They will send an international directory of doctors and medical facilities, a world climate chart, a world immunization chart, a world malaria risk chart, and information on how to protect from malaria. The IAMAT organization asks no fee. However, they will send a card requesting a donation with your package of materials. I find they have the best research information out there and consider this step a must in the initial step of planning a remote trip.

For other professional assistance with consultation and immunizations for travelers, contact

www.passporthealthusa.com

List all the countries you have placed on your itinerary. Some countries require vaccinations against certain diseases if you traveled previously in a country having those diseases. Start with your immunizations at least two months before your departure. Some may require several injections a month apart. Get the small yellow International Certificate of Vaccination booklet upon receiving your first immunization. Before leaving the doctor's office or clinic, check to make sure the doctor signed the booklet, specified the immunization, and stamped the book with the date. If you lose the book while traveling, you may need a replacement immunization without proof of previous inoculation. Protect your immunization book as you would your money. Better yet, scan the entire booklet before you leave home and email the scan to yourself. That way you can keep a copy of the book in a safe place at home.

To familiarize yourself with the health risks and dangers of a given region, spend some time reading guidebooks. Read several, not just the one you bought. Copy the pages of risks and illnesses that pertain to your trip instead of taking the entire book with you. You may never need to look at the material while away, but it is good to have it for reference. If you suddenly do not feel well or you develop symptoms of an illness after visiting a small village in the jungle, your photocopied list of illnesses will help you decide whether you need to find a clinic.

### *FOOD AND WATER*

Consumption of local food and water can affect your health. Where you travel will regulate how much caution to use, concerning your health and diet. For additional details, consult Chapter Seven, Food and Water.

### *WHERE TO GO FOR VACCINATIONS*

See your personal doctor if you need a physical before you leave. Often they will have information or suggestions for the best place for international immunizations. People in excellent health can go to a travel clinic or check with their local health department. Travel clinics specialize in keeping vaccines in stock for international travelers and can offer prescriptions for anti-malarial drugs, syringes, and other travel-related prescriptions. In my area, a travel clinic or general physician would charge $160 for a yellow fever vaccine, compared to the health department's cost of sixty dollars. Not all health departments offer international immunizations, so call first. Some travel clinics welcome walk-ins, and you pay per inoculation. Other clinics may have personnel on staff to answer questions and to give advice. Spend time researching which inoculation you prefer, according to side effects, and how many years the immunization remains valid. Some immunizations like typhoid offer a live vaccine and a dead one. Both have different side effects and length of potency and differ in cost. Malarone, the latest drug for malaria prevention, costs about a dollar a day.

### *FIRST-AID KITS/HEALTH SUPPLIES*

Camping and travel stores as well as catalogs offer all sorts of sizes of first-aid kits, or better yet, pack your own (see Appendix).

If you can get a prescription for disposable, sealed, sterile needles and syringes, do it.

For a blood draw, or an injection of antibiotics for a severe infection, you will be able to use your own needles. Several travel outfitters carry first-aid kits that include these. See, for example, *Magellan's Catalog*. In many countries, needles and syringes lack sterilization, and often-used ones may end up as re-packaged and sold as new.

You place yourself at serious risk with used needles and syringes for blood-borne diseases and AIDS. To avoid suspicion of illegal drug use, just mention diabetes if a security guard questions your possession of a couple of needles.

According to newsgroups, as well as other research I have done, carrying needles and syringes across borders and into remote areas presents no problem, but the return home through customs may present serious problems. Have your prescription with you or throw needles and syringes away before returning.

Tampons and contraceptives exist in larger cities. If you do find them, expect poor quality and high prices. Bring what you need to last your entire trip.

Women should bring medication for yeast infections. Antibiotics kill the good bacteria in your system as well as the bad, making you susceptible to yeast infections.

### *US STATE DEPARTMENT TRAVEL ADVISORIES*

The Department of State issues travel advisories concerning serious health conditions but concentrates on security conditions and political situations that may affect US citizens. (See Appendix, Health.)

### *COMMON DISEASES CONTRACTED*

The worry of illness while traveling keeps many people at home. Most illnesses in undeveloped countries do not have clear guidelines for prevention. Taking vacation time and spending huge amounts of money are all part of taking that trip of a lifetime, and no one wants to risk getting sick. Talk to your doctor and visit the web site for the Center for Disease Control and Prevention at www.cdc.gov, or the International Society of Travel Medicine at www.ISTM.org, or the American Society of Tropical Medicine and Hygiene at www.ASTMH.org.

The most common travel ailment, threatening any type of travel, has the name of Montezuma's Revenge or traveler's diarrhea. About forty percent of people traveling in an undeveloped country will get travel-induced diarrhea. Exposure to different strains of the E. coli bacteria (which we all have in our bodies) causes the diarrhea. Protecting ourselves from those unfortunate trips to the bathroom requires following a few guidelines. Wash your hands before eating food or touching your face. Wash your hands with soap and hot water if you can after using the toilet. Avoid all street vendors selling food. Drink only from sealed bottles of water and do not ask for ice cubes in your drink. Make sure all food consumed is thoroughly cooked. Avoid dairy products like ice cream that may not be pasteurized. Avoid shellfish, fresh cut fruit and vegetables, and food left out in the sun all day. Carry antibacterial gel for your hands and use it often. Look for tiny bottles about an inch tall or those with a loop for attaching to belts and straps. Antibiotics can help with infections, but talk to a doctor about which type is best for various conditions.

I always find a doctor in the area where I get sick as I feel they know best what type of problem I am having and can treat it with certainty.

The change of your diet, stress of travel, or emotional stress can cause problems when traveling abroad. Consider Pepto Bismol for cramping and upset stomach. Imodium and Lomotil will stop diarrhea but do not cure the problem. To avoid dehydration, drink plenty of fluids and replenish electrolytes (like sodium and potassium) with powdered products like Gatorade, which you can take with you in powder form.

If fever, chills, blood in your stools, or diarrhea lasts longer than seventy-two hours, find medical attention. A severe form of dysentery can cause permanent damage to the digestive tract if not treated.

One of my children contracted malaria as a teenager while traveling with me in New Guinea, so I am familiar with its horrible symptoms. But I also know how quick the recovery is if malaria is caught early. The bite of the female Anopheles mosquito was responsible for over 200 million cases of malaria and 600,000 deaths in 2010. The symptoms include a cycling fever with chills, muscle aches, and fatigue, all of which reoccur indefinitely if not treated. The best course of action to prevent malaria is to take a course of preventive medication, wear insect repellent, cover your skin with clothing, and sleep with mosquito nets at night.

The most common vaccine-preventable diseases are Hepatitis A and B. Each infects the liver. Hepatitis A comes from ingesting contaminated food and water, and many Americans contract it in resorts and cities. Most cases are mild, with abdominal pain, jaundice, and flu-like symptoms. Hepatitis B normally arises through sexual contact but can also be contracted through infected blood and surgical instruments, used in medical emergencies. Hepatitis C is the most serious of all the strains, and there is no vaccine for it yet, but the series of vaccines for Hepatitis A and B last a lifetime.

Typhoid is another disease picked up from contaminated food and water. Countries where sanitation and sewage systems are under-developed raise a red flag of caution. Symptoms include fever, rash, headache, and intestinal perforation. There are two types of vaccines. The vaccine given through a shot contains dead Salmonella typhoid bacteria and lasts two years, followed by booster shots. The second type, administered orally, contains a live but weakened strain of Salmonella that causes typhoid fever. Mild flu-like symptoms may occur after getting this oral vaccine, but the vaccine is worth it as this oral vaccine lasts five years, followed by a booster.

Dengue fever is caused by the bite of the Aedes mosquito, but most cases are mild with flu-like symptoms. Follow the same precautions for malaria to prevent this disease, because there is no preventive medication or vaccine.

Polio is another infectious disease caused by contaminated food and water. Improvement in hygienic practices and immunization campaigns have eradicated most polio in the world. The Rotary Clubs have spent over a billion dollars toward this goal. Since 1988, polio cases have a decreased by over 99% (from approximately 350,000 cases to 650 reported cases in 2011). If traveling to the three countries that may still have active cases, Nigeria, Pakistan, and Afghanistan, a polio booster is recommended.

Remember to practice safe sex. You want to bring back great memories and stories of your trip, not sexually transmitted diseases. Pack condoms or look for ones with the European kite symbol, showing a heart with lines through it or the CE symbol. Both marks assure that condoms have met with rigorous standards of product testing. Contact from oil-based products such as massage oil, suntan lotion, and lipstick can damage condoms.

### *MEDICAL TESTS ABROAD*

If you do happen to get sick while traveling and take tests and medication, consider this word of advice. Bring the results of the tests from the doctor and copies of all medications listed by the doctor back home with you. While traveling in New Guinea, my daughter came down with malaria. Having researched the disease, I recognized the symptoms as soon as they appeared. A simple blood test confirmed this, and she took a medication that kills the disease in the bloodstream. However, malaria can move into the liver, if not treated.

The Infectious Disease Clinic in Kansas City would not give her the medication to kill the disease in the liver because we had no proof that she had even had malaria. Her blood tests came back normal, and we had no proof of her taking the medication in New Guinea. Even the CDC could do nothing for her, which meant symptoms could recur many times throughout her lifetime. After many phone calls, trying to find a doctor that could help, and almost making the decision to travel to Mexico where we knew we could get help, someone suggested the doctor in charge of pediatrics at the Kansas University Hospital. This oriental man, about seventy years old, had treated thousands of cases of malaria in his home country of Taiwan. He gave my daughter the medication to treat the liver without hesitation and now, many years later, she is still in good health.

### *STRESS*

A stranger in a strange land. You have fought the battles of fear, money concerns, and the shock of relatives and friends after telling them of your plans. Now you come face-to-face with the challenge. You begin to sense the isolation far from the known comforts of home. (See Chapter Twelve, Culture Shock.)

### *JET LAG*

Crossing several time zones in an airplane can cause jet lag. The time difference disrupts our body clock. This affects our blood pressure, heartbeat, and body temperature. A temporary disorientation can result, and may include mental and physical fatigue. Reduced oxygen pressure causes mental and physical problems similar to those caused by drinking. Cabin pressurization causes low humidity, resulting in dehydration. Alcohol can create similar effects, compounding the fatigue of jet lag. Sitting in a seat for long periods causes discomfort and excessive swelling of the feet. Altitude and pressure changes at every stop upset the body's systems. Lack of sleep, excessive eating, drinking, or poor physical condition do not cause jet lag but help make the symptoms worse. Symptoms can include loss of short-term mental clarity, upset patterns of sleep, general fatigue, and lack of appetite. To prevent jet lag, do not drink alcohol while in the air. Drink lots of water or juice, though, and avoid caffeine. Try to get up and walk around on long flights. Pre-arranging a hotel for the first night or two after landing helps to alleviate the stress of finding a place after the confusion of immigration, customs, and dealing with your luggage. An unknown hotel is not as helpful as one familiar with your expectations and which is easy to locate when tired and confused. Check out nojetlag.com to understand the symptoms. Some fortunate people never suffer from culture shock or jet lag. Do not let the temporary symptoms scare you away from travel.

***TOILETS***

The toilet situation for common sit-down toilets changes depending on distance from cities with sewers. In many parts of the world, toilets do not exist, and people use outhouses or nature for relief. The Turkish toilet in Indonesia, called a mandi, consists of a porcelain piece in the floor with a hole in the middle. There are indentations for your feet, so you know where to stand. You squat with precision while trying to balance. To flush, you pour water from a nearby bucket into the hole, or there may be a chain to pull while you flush with water.

Toilet paper either does not exist, costs too much, or feels like construction paper. In Moslem countries, people use a bucket of water for washing with the left hand.

Therefore, you never shake hands using your left hand. In the more primitive areas of New Guinea, everyone hides behind the nearest tree and uses leaves for cleaning up after.

When I travel, I buy tiny little packets of tissue. In New Guinea I had to dig a small hole first to have somewhere to bury the tissue. In more developed countries and all over Europe, you will find a bidet, along with a toilet. You straddle it and wash.

In many parts of the world, the sewer systems do not handle toilet paper. For example, in Mexico all paper items go into the trash container beside the toilet even if the toilet looks modern and flushes. Paper products cannot go down these primitive sewer systems. Places accommodating Westerners will have a wastebasket nearby for paper products.

### *LAUNDRY*

Laundromats may not exist abroad. Plan to wash your clothes in basins, buckets, rivers, or the shower.

When I travel, I never worry about laundry soap (just one more thing to pack). I take a bar of soap and store it in a two-piece soap dish and use the bar for the dual purpose of washing myself and washing my laundry.

See the packing chapter for my recommendations on synthetic types of clothing that are easy to wash and dry within hours.

I pack a ten-foot length of thin rope, useful as a laundry line or to hold a bag together that has broken. Include four or five clothespins or large safety pins.

### *SUN*

Sunburns do not have to be part of a vacation; remember that binge tanning is the quickest way to get skin cancer. To protect yourself from sunburn, cover your body with clothing, a hat, sunglasses, and sunscreen. Do not use tanning oils. They magnify the sun's rays and reduce nature's sweat, designed to keep you cool.

Prolonged exposure to the sun can damage skin. Exposed skin, lips, eyes, and feet need attention.

First-degree burns can turn into third degree burns without warning. A diabetic friend and I went kayaking in Costa Rica, before spending some time viewing the tree sloths.

A few hours on the river and exploring nature caused my friend a trip to the doctor for treatment for third degree burns because we had completely forgotten to apply sunblock after getting wet in the kayak.

Sun reflecting off sand, water, and snow can cause damage to the cornea, resulting in snow-blindness. Use sunglasses.

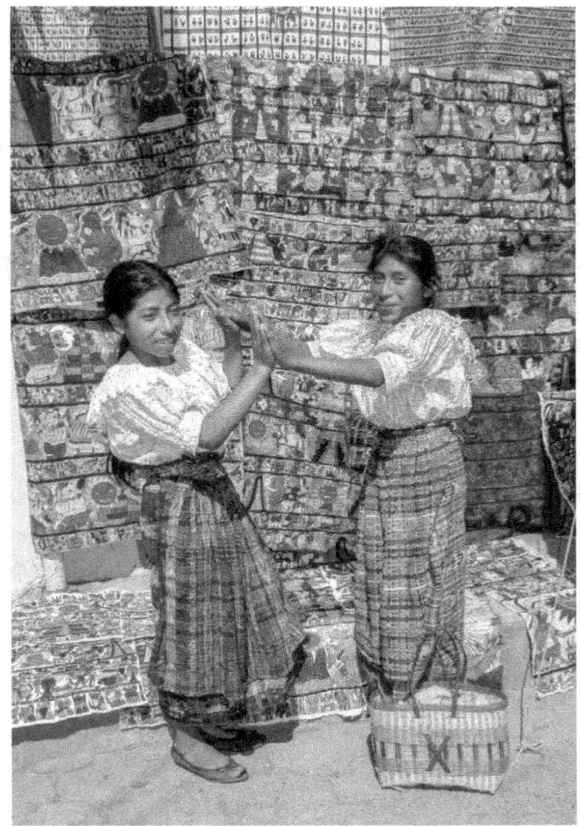

*7. Girls, taking a break from selling, Guatemala*

### ***ALTITUDE SICKNESS***

Acute Mountain Sickness results from a combination of reduced air pressure and lower oxygen levels at high altitudes. Climbing faster to higher altitudes accelerates your chances of getting AMS. Pushing hard and a speedy climb increase symptoms. Living near sea level or having had the illness increases the chances of acquiring AMS. Symptoms, even if mild, can affect the lungs, muscles, heart, and nervous system.

The signs of altitude sickness include headache, shortness of breath with exertion, nausea, rapid pulse, fatigue, loss of appetite, lethargy, dizziness, and sleep problems. Serious AMS might develop with no warning and can lead to death. Symptoms include cough with blood, bluish color of the skin, chest tightness, severe headache, vomiting, breathlessness at rest, confusion, lack of balance or inability to walk, and decreased consciousness. AMS occurs because less oxygen reaches the muscles and the brain at high altitude (above 8,000 feet or 2,400 meters), which requires the lungs and heart to work harder. Symptoms can develop in twenty-four hours. Skiers, trekkers, and travelers should use caution. A general physician will prescribe Diamox to use at the first signs of sickness. Use caution with any drugs as they all have side effects. Diamox requires you to drink extra fluids.

The treatment for AMS takes time. Rest for one or two days at the present altitude and take common painkillers or ask around for local remedies. In Peru, a local remedy involved drinking mate de coca, a tea, made from coca leaves and sold in cafes. People buy coca leaves in *tiendas,* or market stalls, for about five dollars a kilo. Indians chew coca leaves to dull the sensation of cold and hunger, a legal activity there. The alkalinity from ash or bicarbonate of soda releases the stimulant in the leaves. The priority, in severe AMS, consists of descending as soon as possible to a lower altitude. You may hear of numerous drug treatments that enable you to ascend or avoid descending, but beware of taking these. Drugs like Diamox and Dexamethasone work well at reducing the symptoms but hide the warning signs, and people taking these drugs have suffered severe and fatal AMS.

To prevent AMS, avoid sedatives and alcohol, drink extra fluids to replace lost moisture when you breathe in cold, dry mountain air, and ascend with care. Take numerous rest stops.

### *MOTION SICKNESS*

Signals reaching your brain from your eye, inner ears, and muscle sensors can sometimes malfunction and cause motion sickness. For many, the nausea goes away with time. A prescription for scopolamine, a small patch to wear behind the ear, works for some. Anti-nausea wristbands have a small bead built into them that applies a gentle pressure to relieve symptoms of motion sickness. The band helps symptoms occurring in planes, cars, trains, and boats. Patches, wristbands, antihistamines, and ginger all work well if taken before the problems begin.

While sailing in the Caribbean, we bought cases of ginger ale and ginger snaps. Dramamine and Meclizine work well but cause drowsiness unless you buy the non-drowsy type. Seasick while sailing off the shores of Puerto Rico on a thirty-six-foot boat, I found it helped to lie down. People say it helps to keep your eyes on the horizon and face forward. Cruising the Straits of Magellan on the Terra Australis, I decided to try the wristbands. For me, they worked great. Contact www.biobands.com

### *EXPOSURE EXTREMES*

Heat and cold extremes can cause the body's temperature regulation system to shut down. Hypothermia results from severe wind-chill factors or exposure to low water temperatures for extended periods. The body cannot warm itself, so the body temperature drops. Another person or animal can help insulate the victim of hypothermia until help arrives. When the skin freezes, it dies (frostbite). With sunstroke or heatstroke, the body stops cooling itself, which causes the body temperature to elevate. Loss of consciousness, brain damage, and even death can result. Someone collapsing from the heat needs immediate care. Until help arrives, shade the person, bathe him/her with cool water, and offer fluids and acetaminophen to lower the body temperature.

### *CARE OF THE FEET*

Proper care of the feet prevents bothersome and painful foot problems. Precautions will alleviate blisters, infections, athlete's foot, and hook-worm infections. Break in your shoes well before a trip. As soon as a blister develops, cut a donut-shaped piece of moleskin, and attach over it. Puncture blisters with a sterile needle at the base, put pressure on the blister, dry, and bandage it. Wear flip-flops or thongs in showers to prevent infections but never wear these for trekking.

Protect your feet from sharp edges of rocks, tangling vines, broken glass, snakes slithering across your path, insects, and spiders. I remember the spider rule quite well, as Luis (my guide in the Amazon) told me not to scream, move, or sweat when a tarantula crossed over my boot and up my leg while we were putting up mosquito nets for the night.

Sun and air help your feet. Remember to change your socks often. Allow your feet to dry after washing, and apply foot powder to minimize bacteria.

My first experience with hiking boots was while trekking in the Amazon with my daughter. Our hiking boots became tangled in a nest of roots and vines. We looked at each other, and as if reading each other's mind, yelled to the treetops, "Thank you, Eddie Bauer!"

### *CUTS, BITES AND STINGS*

If not kept clean and dry, cuts and abrasions in the tropics cause infections. Sometimes and unexpected incident will cause abrasions. A female orangutan jumped on me, causing me to fall backwards into a poisonous plant in the jungles of Borneo. For days I scratched. In Ethiopia, several tribal women decided to initiate me into their village by pounding many bronze bracelets around my arm, using rocks to secure them. The edges of the metal cut my wrist. Several times a day I used boiled water to clean the abrasions in order to prevent infection. Minor scrapes heal better when exposed to the air. Clean every day with soap and hot sterile water. Find suture kits or carry butterfly bandages.

The most serious insect bite is the mosquito carrying malaria. Contact IAMAT for their malarial risk chart and instructions on how to protect against malaria and watch for symptoms. Symptoms take three weeks before they start to appear. Spending several days in a large city in New Guinea while arranging for our jungle trek, my daughter never thought about malaria. A nice hotel gave us plenty of protection at night, or so we thought. After three weeks of intense jungle trekking, Katherine came down with severe headaches, followed by phases of fever and then chills. I knew the signs signaled malaria but did not expect to see symptoms so soon. She had met with that dreaded mosquito in the city of Jayapura before we even entered the jungle.

Most cases of malaria can be treated if caught soon enough. Prevent it by protecting exposed skin with DEET insect repellent or other repellants on the market. The higher the percentage of DEET, the more protection offered.

Research the different chemicals for repellents and the symptoms after use. Recommendations suggest washing DEET off the skin each night, but this is not practical when sleeping in a jungle. Permethrin sprays help ward off mosquitoes when used on clothing and tents.

You can also buy clothes and bedding treated with insect repellent. Natrapel insect repellent has no chemicals so that children can use it. Check www.campmor.com. Simple insect bites run the risk of infection if not treated or not kept clean, or if scratched open.

A scratched-open mosquito bite on my toe developed into an infected, red, and swollen sore for two weeks in Ecuador. A Quechua chief gave me some Dragon's Blood (red sap used for every internal and external medical problem in their village), which dried the sore in two days.

Hydrocortisone or Benadryl cream stops the itching of prickly heat, hives, allergies, and bites.

The generic drug Loratadine, also known as Claritin, works by blocking a substance in the body called histamine and helps decrease allergy and itching symptoms. The twelve-hour sustained release tablets work well for a sudden attack of itchy insect bites.

My daughter Katherine used it after she woke one morning with hundreds of fleabites. The night before, she had been reading by flashlight in the fresh-laid grass of our New Guinea jungle hut.

Get commercial products made for stings of bees, wasps, and jellyfish if you travel where stings could occur.

Papaya enzyme tablets form a paste for stings. If allergic to stings, take your medication with you.

### *TICKS AND LEECHES*

Ticks can attack when you are trekking in forested areas, but alcohol, petroleum products, and tweezers remove them. Chiggers cause some fierce itching. Sulfur or insect repellents will keep them away.

Leeches look awful, and your first instinct to tear them off could lead to problems, as this just increases the bleeding. Leeches produce an anti-coagulant substance in the blood. Try to remove them, instead, with a lit match, tobacco, salt, or insect repellent. The leeches in northern Thailand measure less than an inch long and like to squish into your shoes through the eyelets. Soon, a wet sensation moves between your toes. Leeches appear in vast quantities after a rain and even rain ponchos do not keep them away. Unaware of their love for warm blood for lunch, I screamed after finding that the burning sensation on my knee came from a shiny oozy worm.

### *YOUR PHYSICAL CONDITION*

Traveling consumes your resources. It requires energy, passion, and a sense of wellbeing to add fuel to your regular activities.

About a month or more before a walking trek, I fill my backpack with the equivalent weight and walk as much as I can with the pack and the boots I plan to wear on the trip. If I travel to the tropics, I soak a lot in Jacuzzis or saunas to get myself prepared for heat and humidity. The climate may differ from what your body enjoys.

Climate and altitude will influence your preparation and comfort. Acclimating to a new climate takes time. Allow yourself that flexibility.

### *BROKEN BONES, SPRAINS AND STRAINS*

Many injuries result from fatigue or carelessness. Watch your step. Follow rules of the road when trekking. Hiking boots will help in those areas of loose rock or tangles of roots in the jungle. Rest when you find you are slipping into carelessness.

Sprains consist of injuries to the ligaments or fibers that hold the bones in place or to the tissues surrounding the joints.

A quick twist can tear or misshape the ligaments or tissue. A painful joint that turns black and blue could indicate a sprain. Use compresses or elastic bandages and elevate the area.

Remember I.C.E.: immobilize, compress, elevate. Determining the difference between a fracture and a sprain requires an X-ray. Seek medical assistance when in doubt.

### *SWIMMING AND BATHING*

Swim in chlorinated pools or salt water and never in fresh standing or flowing water unless local health authorities or the villagers recommend bathing there. Lakes, streams, rivers, and even deep water may be infested by tiny worms called bilharzias that can invade openings in your body. They attach themselves to your bladder or intestines and produce large numbers of eggs.

Snails, living in stagnant water, support another dangerous disease called schistosomiasis. If you or your clothes get wet, dry off as soon as you can. Do not put your head under water when swimming near populated bathing areas. Dive or snorkel in open water, away from polluted areas.

Bathing facilities can range from hot showers to buckets of ice-cold water to rivers. Most hostels have shared toilet and shower facilities, used by everyone on the floor. They may have just cold water.

Whenever I get into a simmering, hot shower, memories of the many cold ones come to mind. Traveling to Third and Fourth world countries will make you appreciate hot showers.

Available water determines bathing in remote areas. Rivers, streams, and wells might offer options. Ask your guide or the locals if the rivers have the bilharzia worms. If they do, use a bucket of boiled water for a sponge bath. Do not fret if locals watch as you bathe. People want to know about your routine, perhaps different from their own. They will try to hide behind trees, but you will suspect their presence. I have never had any problems.

I leave underclothing on, or I use a sarong like the locals in most countries. Take a piece of fabric wide enough and long enough to cover your private parts. Find sarongs in markets for less than five dollars.

Wash and pour water over yourself with the sarong on. Slip into clean clothes or a dry sarong and hang the wet sarong to dry. Guys might like to wear a lightweight swimsuit, which will serve the same purpose. A sarong serves many more functions, like that of a towel or a light sheet in rooms with air-conditioners set on high.

***TRAVEL INSURANCE***

Specialized travel insurance offers a variety of coverage. Call your insurance or travel agent, check for ads in camping and travel magazines, or see the appendix for a few listings of companies offering insurance.

Trip cancellation and trip interruption insurance costs vary and require research. This insurance covers any penalties due to cancellation and enables you to obtain a refund under certain conditions. It may also pay for the cost of taking an alternate route, should your plans change.

Different policies contain unique clauses and coverage. They may include (for your targeted country) compensation for death, serious illness/injury to you or a traveling companion, default or bankruptcy of a travel provider, airline or other travel-related operators, and, or even terrorist acts or threats.

Medical evacuation insurance arranges for air ambulance, doctors and/or nurses, life-support facilities, immigration and custom services. Serious illness or injury may require a life flight evacuation to the nearest large city for emergency treatment.

Even a medical flight home can cost over $50,000. Medical evacuation insurance has high costs as an added rider on the most comprehensive policies. Under most conditions, you would not feel too sick or injured to travel by commercial airliner.

Any city with air service can get someone to a larger city with an adequate hospital, and faster than getting an air ambulance.

I would recommend medical evacuation insurance if you will be traveling to a dangerous area or to areas without airline service. Read the fine print on your policy before signing up. The remote areas I travel to do not have roads, let alone air service. Sometimes this insurance can cost an extra fifty dollars or more for a month-long trip.

For frequent travelers, insurance from MASA could offer year-round coverage worldwide for a monthly premium. Call 800-423-3226.

Even a short cruise to the Bahamas requires thinking about travel insurance. Three hours after we left the port, the Captain announced the ship would return to the port because a passenger had a serious illness.

A travel insurance policy holder asked me the next morning if that family had to pay for the loss of those six hours of fuel. You may wish to ask this question when buying insurance.

We take for granted the Western-level healthcare available in First World countries. Your travel may take you hundreds of miles from reputable medical facilities.

Prepare for emergencies in remote locations. Beware of exclusions in your travel insurance policy for undesirable risks, like most risky sports (mountain climbing, motor sports, and diving).

Traveler's health insurance will cover most medical costs while you are traveling. Your own personal policy will not cover emergency treatment while abroad. Medicare does not cover international travel.

Travel insurance does not pay expenses until you make a claim and include your receipts.

In remote areas of the world, health care might cost little or nothing.

A special policy for the sole purpose of traveling (traveler's health insurance) lists premiums starting at three dollars a day and higher, depending on where and how long you travel.

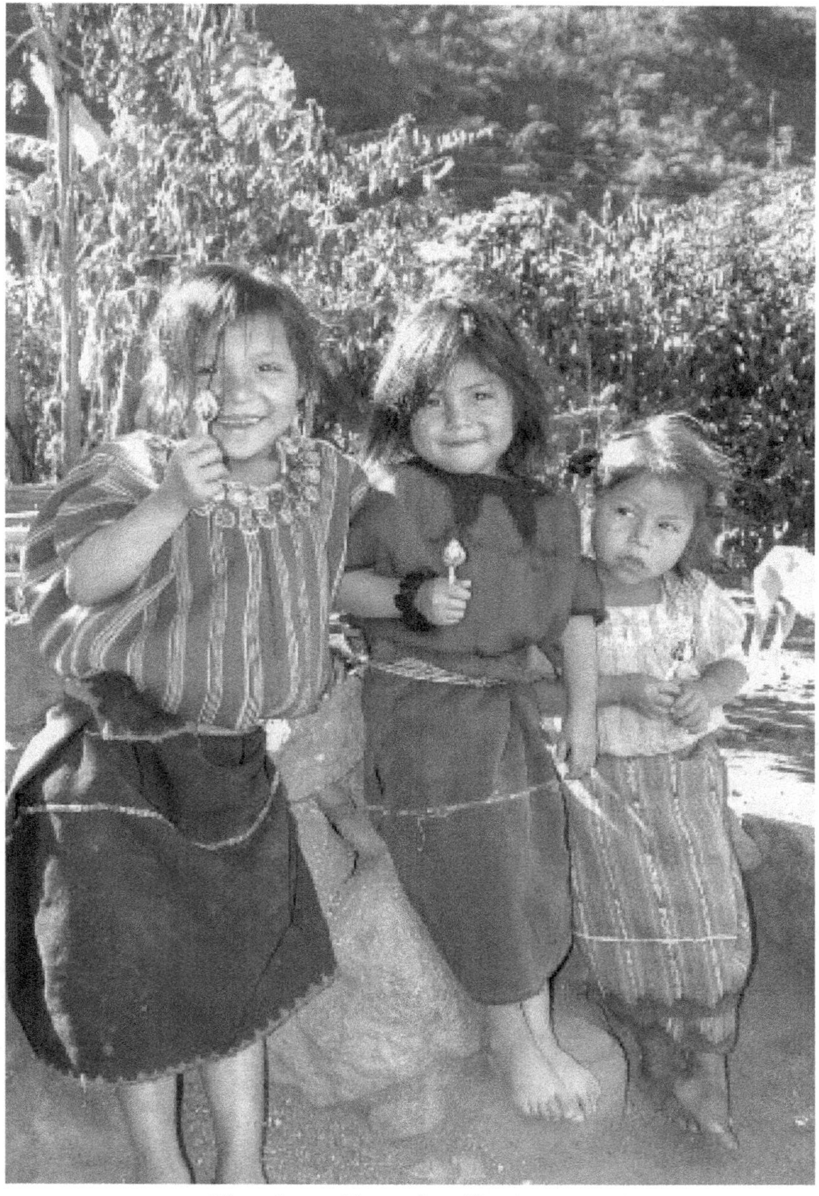

8. Showing off candy gift, Guatemala

# Chapter 6: transportation

*"A wise traveler has no fixed plans and is not intent upon arriving."* Lao Tzu

***MANY OPTIONS***

The first segment of your trip often includes plane travel. Once you deplane, you will have to make decisions as to how you will travel within the country. You can reach even the most remote destinations one way or another. Research will yield ideas on how to reach villages.

Traveling as locals do will offer the most intriguing mode of transport. Your journey may involve staying within reach of roads but seeking adventures off the road.

Some of my favorites include assisting in building a bamboo raft for a wet downriver trip on the border of Burma, bouncing on the back of an elephant in northern Thailand, and enduring the wooden saddle, hiding the camel's hump in the Sahara.

No matter how difficult the terrain may look on a map, you can still get there. Consider the alternate modes of transportation within the country. Ground travel enables you to enjoy the country and its people.

Traveling on the ground bridges the gap between you and the country, whereas air travel may cause you to miss important sights between airports.

***AIRLINES***

The first two places to check for inexpensive flights include the Internet and the travel section of the New York Times or the Los Angeles Times.

The resources on the Internet will answer most questions you may have. Check online resources that include money-saving, simple auctions like www.skyauction.com or www.priceline.com where you can bid on airline flights and even hotels and restaurants.

Find helpful air-pass programs at www.oneworldalliance.com. Check options within alternate sites such as www.airtimetable.com and www.staralliance.com. It is helpful to consult online newsletters like www.smartertravel.com. These resources provide valuable travel tips. For an airport transportation guide, try www.salkinternational.com. It shows transportation to the city from every airport in the world.

Get to major hotels using this guide. Wonder why airlines say the flight is on time when the plane is not at the gate?

There are several sites to check the statistics of how often a flight is on time like www.flightcaster.com and
www.airfarewatchdog.com.

Comfortable clothing, including layers to add or remove, makes airline travel more inviting. The temperatures you will encounter make it imperative that you wear short sleeves and have progressively heavier pieces to slip on over them.

Place everything you think you might use such as music, favorite headphones, reading material, snacks, and a pen in a small bag. During the flight, you can reach under your seat for the bag.

Copy your passport information onto a piece of scratch paper so you can fill out the customs and immigration forms without digging through bags stored above.

Some airlines provide toothbrushes and slippers. Take advantage of exercises shown on your video monitors if provided, or get up and walk around, and do a few deep knee bends, etc.

The best investment for long trips, the travel neck pillow, helps keep neck muscles relaxed and keeps the head from falling forward when nodding off. Refrain from too many salty snacks, which can cause swelling of your feet, making it difficult to put on your shoes.

Drink lots of water, not coffee, tea, or alcohol. These diuretics increase the body's dehydration. To avoid irritated eyes, remove contact lenses. Use a skin moisturizer for dry skin and lips. An inactive body makes digesting food difficult, so avoid overeating.

Sitting upright and remaining inactive for long periods affect blood circulation and the ability to relax your muscles. These exercises will help you on your next flight. Copy and print them:

Neck Roll: Relax your shoulders, drop your chin to chest and roll your head in circles in both directions five times each.

Knee Lifts: While contracting your thigh muscle, lift leg with knee bent. Repeat twenty times for each leg.

Forward Flex: Hold your stomach in and keep both feet on the floor. Bend forward at a relaxed pace and walk your hands down the front of your legs toward the ankles. Sit up after holding the stretch for fifteen seconds.

Ankle Circles: Lift both feet off the floor and draw a circle with your toes. Move toes in opposite directions for fifteen seconds, and then change directions.

Shoulder Roll: Hunch your shoulders in a circular motion from downward, to backward, then upward, and then forward.

Knee Raise: Put your hands on the armrests, lift your knees together, hold five seconds, and repeat ten times.

Foot Lift for Heels: Let the balls of your feet touch the floor. Lift your heels as high as you can and hold for thirty seconds.

Foot Lift for Toes: Leave your heels on the floor and lift your toes, pointing upward as high as possible and hold for thirty seconds.

Leg March: While seated, contract your thigh muscles and march in place for thirty seconds.

Back Arch: Move your shoulders forward while arching your torso backward.

Then move your shoulders backward and your torso forward. This relieves lower back pain.

### *COURIERS*

Another method of travel involves courier travel. Courier companies work with independent travelers.

They use the traveler's name, which allows them to use the traveler's allotment for checked luggage to ship documents or parcels.

This way, they move packages faster than other methods. Packages sent as freight sit on docks in crates waiting forever to go through customs.

You may have difficulty finding courier travel information, and few companies offer courier services as they once did because of security measures and travel restrictions.

### *TRAINS*

To experience a country, ride the train. Trains offer varying degrees of comfort or survivability, depending upon the country. Europe has economical, comfortable, and clean, rail travel.

In the rest of the world, not including North America, the journey on trains can provide future dinner conversations. Trains in India range from first class to third class. However, third class in India feels and smells more like a freight car with as many people packed in as possible.

Men without legs would scoot along the floor, whisking away trash under seats and expecting payment.

Women with small children encouraged them to sing and dance in the aisles for payment. Children with serene faces slept in the aisles while others stepped over them, treating them like mounds of garbage.

Security guards left the trains soon after leaving the large cities, so beggars came aboard at every stop. Some trains defy description. Research your mode of travel.

Traveling can be a nightmare, with unbearable sanitation, crowded floors without seats, bugs crawling everywhere, potential thieves, intense heat, and no food or water.

The local train to Machu Picchu, Peru has the features of one of the train trips I would recommend.

The tourist train gets there faster but lacks character. The local train greets each small village, allowing people to load and unload vegetables and chickens.

However, tourists are not allowed to ride the local train any more. In Ecuador men ride on the roof. The roof feels cooler, less crowded, and offers vistas for miles in every direction.

The trains I have traveled on in South America and Asia make stops at every little village along the way, and within minutes, children fill the cars hawking bowls of candy, breads, tiny brown-paper-wrapped cones of rice, and sometimes meat on sticks. Climbing through windows and over seats, they are still selling goods as the train begins to move. Travelers reach out of windows and grab bananas from bowls, belonging to women standing too close to the train.

A comfortable, air-conditioned train runs over the Copper Canyon into Creel, Mexico. The train climbs the canyon, offering glimpses of beauty, surpassing that of the Grand Canyon. Riding on the roof of a train beats all my train experiences. From Guayaquil to Quito in Ecuador, one can ride on the roof, reap the benefits of the view, make friends with those beside you, and see firsthand the villagers, selling food to passengers below at the many stops along the way.

Check your guidebook for approximate schedules and train passes, but remember that guidebooks often have outdated schedules. Check with the internet or at the local station for accurate schedules. While traveling throughout southern China, I used the train schedule from the internet and found the times and days accurate. Check www.CNVOL.com. Many destinations like Europe offer a variety of rail passes based upon age group and length of travel. Trains in

Western Europe offer the best way to travel if you have the time. The grand Orient Express has the best reputation for train travel, with a five-night trip from Istanbul to Venice costing a mere $10,000.

For world travel, check www.railpasses.com, and for USA travel, check www.amtrak.com.

### *BUSES*

Bus travel, the most accessible form of transportation, moves people from sunsets in small villages to skyscrapers along the Rhine. Buses do not require reservations, cost less than air travel, and go everywhere.

The size of the bus and level of comfort varies even in the same city, depending on the bus line. Buses can range in comfort from offering movies on television screens, free meals, air conditioning, and soft, cushy seats to being nothing more than overcrowded people pens.

Crowding means five people, two chickens, and a kilo of homegrown vegetables sandwiched into two filthy, dirty seats. The more remote the area, the less quality you will find and the more overcrowding. However, those unforgettable experiences fill our minds and hearts with memories when we return home. People smile at you; you may hear a song.

The woman in the next seat shares her one snack on a twelve-hour ride with you. The intimate contact you have in this kind of situation is certainly memorable. If anyone on the bus speaks English, consider that person your friend, since he, while practicing English, will share local knowledge with you.

*Rocky*, *narrow*, and *dangerous* are words that describe road conditions in Third and Fourth World countries. Breakdowns and flat tires occur often. Luggage goes on the roof of buses; anything alive goes inside. When the bus stops, watch who gets off and what luggage the boy who sits up on the roof removes. Lock all bags, take out all valuables, and put them in your daypack, keeping it with you on your lap at all times. By taking the bus, you will get to know the landscape, all the little villages along the way, and the wonderful people you meet inside, squished beside you. Check sites like www.eurolines.com for European bus passes, www.mexperience.com for Mexican bus information, www.greyhound.com for US information, and for worldwide travel, www.statravel.co.nz/asia-bus-rail.htm.

### AUTOMOBILES

Renting cars and driving your own automobile have advantages and disadvantages. Traveling by car provides comfort and privacy. You will go where and when you desire. For either situation, you will need to familiarize yourself with the rules of driving cars in each country. From the U.S., the easiest long-distance trips to foreign places head north to Canada and south to Mexico.

Travel to either has few complications. However, both require some research about international driver's licenses and rules at border crossings. You will have the option of traveling to hard-to-find places, but beware of your status as a wealthy tourist, a target for theft. Border crossings will challenge the tourist, as he will need all the proper documents to be able to cross for both the vehicle and himself. Making reservations for overseas rentals saves money and alleviates hassles with language barriers if done in advance. Economy cars are scarce, so rent them well in advance.

Double-check all rules, such as whether you can take the car into another country or if you can drop it off in a different location from where you picked it up. Read your contract carefully for options, gas refills, insurance, and mileage limits. Valid car insurance for the country you visit requires planning. Your insurance from home will not cover you in a foreign country. In Mexico, for example, you need Mexican insurance and without it, you may go to jail if you get into an accident. You could be stuck there for several weeks. Check www.fuelcostcalculator.com to estimate the cost and amount of gasoline required for a trip. Before a trip, download the free app from www.gasbuddy.com to find the cheapest fuel prices while traveling.

### TAXIS

Vans, buses, trucks, rickshaws, scooters, three-wheeled tuk-tuks, and cars qualify for the name of taxi. Taxis may not have meters, in which case you need to establish the price before you enter the car. The first time I was scammed was in Bali. The driver wanted 200,000 Rupiah, or twenty dollars, to take me about an hour away, but when I got within ten minutes of the hotel, he stopped on a one-way street and said he wanted more money. He pointed to the one-way street sign and said it would take him a long time to go around that area of the city. He told me to get out and walk if I wanted. I gave in to his demand for the additional 30,000, or three dollars.

At transportation terminals (train, bus, or plane), taxi drivers want to take you to their favorite hotel. They will drive straight to the hotel where they get a commission and downplay any other choice of hotel. Drivers use the phrase, "That hotel of your choice is closed, and my brother has a newer one." They will go in with you as you check in and get a tip or a cash commission for bringing you there. Do not fall prey to intimidation. Insist they take you to one of the places on your list. You agreed on a fare before you entered the taxi, so it should not cost you more to go to your choice of locations.

The thing about foreign travel that intimidates me begins at the airport. Faced with a shouting arena outside immigration and customs, I feel like an octopus with arms pulled in every direction. Men yell, they pull at your shirt-sleeves, and some grab your bags. Unless I have accommodations already reserved for my first night, I stand back until most of the arriving passengers have left, and just a few taxis remain. In peace, I can ask a driver if he recognizes the name of my hotel choice, and I ask his price. One tip that eliminates all these worries is to have your hotel arrange to pick you up at the airport using a sign with your name on it. Cool!

### *HITCHHIKING*

Hitchhiking has risks, but many use it as a form of travel more often with safer results in parts of the world other than in the United States. It requires using your instincts. If you are uncomfortable with the driver, do not get into the car. Women alone have greater risks of encountering problems but have a better chance of getting a ride than men traveling alone. In remote areas, only trucks use the roads. In Ecuador, my daughter and I found our ride on the roof of a train, which stopped for no apparent reason in some unexpected small town. We stood at a crossroads and waited for some vehicle to show up. Every bus that came by went in the wrong direction. A truck with thousands of green bananas in the back stopped and picked up about ten Indians waiting with us. We had yelled "Riobamba" at every bus that slowed, so the Indians knew our destination, and they yelled "Riobamba" when the banana truck showed up, motioning for us to join them.

I had seen rowdy men, stumbling toward the bus stop and fewer buses came to a stop here, so riding on the back of a banana truck looked as practical as any alternative. The ride produced memory-making stories to share later. Sitting on thousands of bananas, we listened to songs, shared snacks (they had never tasted almonds or raisins), and when it started to rain, we all huddled together under a heavy tarp. People in Third and Fourth World countries expect these experiences. Often, while I have been traveling in foreign countries, trucks have stopped for me and offered rides for no payment. I donate to their gas fund or share some of my fruit with them. As a matter of fact, I carry fruit for just this purpose.

### *MOTORCYCLES AND BICYCLES*

Bikes and motorbikes have tremendous advantages if you wish to observe the elements of the landscape and the people. You develop closeness with new surroundings and new terrain, while meeting the challenge of it, too. Traveling from one place to another with all your gear requires much of your energy, and arriving at your destination rewards your patience and courage.

Traveling by either bike or motorcycle demands research and thought. The right equipment, clothing, and spare parts will alleviate most minor problems. In some countries like Vietnam, hundreds of bicycles (simple and inexpensive to repair) intimidate pedestrians attempting to cross streets or enter sidewalks. Pedals of bikes, being transported from village to village, poke into legs of passengers on boats, trains, and buses.

Travelers lug their rented bikes up flights of hotel stairs for security at night. I have rented bicycles, and I find them within my budget, in good condition, and available anywhere. Cycling helps you get out and explore a city, and because bicycles represent a humble form of transportation, their use makes meeting people effortless. Motorcycle rentals cover greater distances and can go where the roads disappear. Packing an easy-to-carry tent, sleeping bag, and stove grants you permission to indulge in the out-of-doors. Consider buying simple tools like a pump for tires.

### *WALKING AND MISCELLANEOUS TRAVEL*

In Third and Fourth World countries, when you have traveled as far as you can go by public transport (be it bus, truck or canoe), then you walk or use other forms, for which you pay a guide. In northern Thailand, I took a train, rode in the back of a truck to a drop-off point to enter the jungle, and trekked for several days to different tribal villages. A few villages had elephants available which I could hire to ride to the next village for little money. As an elephant carries you through rice fields during planting season, a group of villagers might motion for you to join in the planting. Through such interaction, your appreciation will grow for these villagers, subsisting on the land. Prepare for all the village children to appear. You look as strange to them as they do to you. With walking, you appreciate the movement of the land.

The opportunity to ride an ancient mode of transportation could introduce you to a new culture and way of life. You will begin to relate to the people when you see from your train or bus window how they live, work, and play, or as you bounce along on the top of a camel or elephant. Traveling overland involves more adventure than air travel. It provides you more time to reflect on your trip and your life.

### *BOATS AND CRUISES*

Cruises and larger ships can take you places where roads may not exist, such as islands or rough coasts in Africa or elsewhere. But smaller boats offer many additional options. Dugout canoes, handmade reed boats, outriggers, sailboats, and hundreds of varieties of motorboats simplify your access to water travel. The tranquility of the water creates a peaceful trip, whether canoeing in the Amazon or sailing the Nile. In many places, water provides the best highway to get from point A to point B. Research your destination. Find out if you will utilize some form of water travel because you will need to prepare for its potential and for challenging situations. Once in the Amazon our motorized canoe fought a rainstorm for four hours. The rain ruined our gear and we felt cold and uncomfortable the entire trip.

For several days of ferry travel, you need to read about the accommodations and food available. In remote countries, the kitchen facilities may not meet your standards. In fact, you can count on it. Plan snacks by packing power bars, fruit, nuts, cheese, and canned meat. Take some method of purifying river water. In populated cities, riverboat travel means arriving well before embarkation time, carving out a space for your body, and maintaining it until the boat leaves. These boats pack every square inch of space with people or goods so expect a lot of pushing and shoving. Just maintain confidence and hold your own. Make sure you find space under cover from rain and away from toilets and the kitchen area. You will find river travel fascinating. Boats slow as they pass villages, stopping if they have cargo to unload or if passengers stand on the docks waiting to board. You will find transportation on any large river in the world. Traveling by freighter, though, may cost more than other options.

# Chapter 7: food and shelter

*"A journey is a person in itself; no two are alike. And all plans, safeguards, policies, and coercion are fruitless. We find after years of struggle that we do not take a trip; a trip takes us."* John Steinbeck

***THE ADVENTURE OF EATING***

An element of travel that attracts everyone involves sampling the local food. Exposure to different foods can turn an ordinary trip into a memorable adventure. Check out markets to find foods for sale and watch what other people order in restaurants. Some people have a real affair with the recipes passed from generation to generation, cooked in the traditional manner of the region.

Guidebooks suggest expensive restaurants and budget cafes. I like to find the hidden cafes on back streets where the locals hang out but speak no English. If the place looks clean and busy with locals, I figure it may offer excellent value and safety. I order a couple of things on the menu just in case one is too spicy or not to my taste. I enjoy supporting the local owners. Discovering diverse food varieties helps the new adventurer acclimate to his new environment. The crunchy beetles in Thailand might just charm the socks off your feet. They taste delicious!

Using a phrasebook will help you select foods that sound enjoyable, after you review the menu. Check the chapter on food in a guidebook. The research you do before your trip will pay off with finding restaurants and negotiating prices. When you plan to look for a place to eat, take your copy of menu translations and consult locations in your handy guidebook.

Businesses and restaurants close from noon to two PM in many parts of the world. The main meal of the day comes before this.

Try to take advantage of this and eat specials of the day to save money. It takes time to find a clean, busy restaurant where your instincts say, "Eat here." Reduce your meals to two a day, which will save you precious travel time and money.

### *STAYING HEALTHY*

To stay healthy while traveling, use caution when consuming food and drinks. Keeping possession of your health while you travel should remain at the top of your priorities.

Remember the rules as your adventure treats you to endless varieties of foods. Stay away from milk products, including ice cream and yogurt in less industrialized countries. We expect pasteurization and homogenization, and raw milk can cause stomach and intestinal aches. Watch for cleanliness, refrigeration, and be on the lookout for rats and roaches. Check your guidebook if you have travelers' diarrhea since different symptoms suggest different remedies. Imodium could work as an instant fix, but Ciprofloxacin, an all-purpose antibiotic, works wonders along with dry food and lots of liquids.

### *FANCY RESTAURANTS OR CAFES*

Traveling in large First World cities will not challenge your health, just your wallet. When eating at the Hilton in Hong Kong, you can savor the oriental flavors of the city or fall back on the trusty old hamburger and drink all the ice water you need. In larger cities all over the world, you will find American chains like Dunkin Donuts, McDonald's, KFC, and Pizza Hut. I will never forget the night I came from an intense jungle trek in the Amazon and felt dirty, hungry, and needing some American food. The owner of the house I rented made a call and half an hour later, a little motorcycle came by with a big red Pizza Hut box strapped on back. Just the smell alone satisfied my taste buds. Such restaurants, or any that cater to the affluent crowd, have clean, sanitary conditions. If your trip is to emphasize your enjoyment of the delicacies of the country you visit, expensive restaurants will give you few worries about health problems. If your budget allows, and spending money on food pleases you, then do not hesitate to find the most talked about and expensive restaurants.

No matter what your budget, ask yourself several questions before ordering. Do I see a clean establishment? Do many people eat here? Should I walk back and peek into the kitchen? The answers to these questions indicate if you can expect safe food, prepared fresh, and served hot for the volume of people coming in.

Neighborhood cafes offer a climate of energy as they bustle with local activity. Check out the table next to you and order what they are having if it looks inviting.

**RULES OF THE TABLE**

Etiquette for the table changes according to the culture you visit. In remote Africa, Asia, and South America, you do not often see eating utensils.

You can carry your own; just make sure you can wash them after eating. Many times, however, you will find a situation where you will offend your hosts by pulling out your own fork.

In case you end up using your hands, use your right hand, as the left hand handles all unsanitary chores. If you receive a bowl of water to dip your fingers in after eating, do not expect a towel for drying.

With nobody around to understand our hesitation to try unusual foods, our apprehension builds.

Immerse yourself in local customs which helps remove false impressions and shows respect. That comfortable cocoon from home will begin to break free as you begin to adjust to the new way foods are offered and served.

Your journey will bring many opportunities, such as invitations to eat with families in their homes. Customs dictate the whys of your invitation. Bargaining in a market begins with laughter, followed by sincere handshakes and offers for dinner.

While trying to find my way to my hotel in a small Papua New Guinea town, a woman helped me to the hotel door.

She then invited me for lunch. Her son smiled and nodded at the same time as she did when I initiated my own offer for them to join me for lunch at the little local place next door, an honor for both parties.

When a host offers food, do not refuse if at all possible. In Mali when a holy woman offered me a ladle of holy water to drink in front of the entire village, I drank the untreated water rather than risk offending her and the chief.

I have learned in one way or another how to explain that I do not eat meat when I travel, for safety's sake. Living with the Tuareg people in the Sahara, I discovered they ate goat meat with no fruit, vegetables, or bread. The tiny, skinned goat laid sliced open in the Sahara sun outside the tent.

My stomach turned thinking about eating that baby goat. Because the elder of the clan saw physical traits in me similar to the Tuaregs, they took no offense in my decline to join them and allowed me to eat my own protein bars.

They viewed me as a Tuareg, maybe ten generations back. Through hand motions I think they told me to go home, gain weight, and then return and eat with them.

### *STREET VENDORS*

These entrepreneurs hang out around the market area or bus and train stations with their street carts, selling a wide variety of foods. They operate day and night. Street vendors can offer an adventurous and cheap way to sample food.

Watch how they prepare the food. Does the person doing the cooking look clean? Inside a restaurant, you never know who cooks the food and how.

Perhaps the meat sat on the counter all day. Vendors have all their cooking ingredients in sight.

Point to spices or vegetables you want more or less of. As a health precaution, I avoid all meat, including fish, when I travel.

Walking by hundreds of street vendors during my travels, I have seen raw meat sitting in the hot sun for hours. The aroma of shish-kabobs grilling is appetizing as you walk by, but I would rather not risk getting sick.

The majority of people living in undeveloped countries eat their meals from street vendors and never have a sick day.

I once ate fresh fried doughnuts and homemade potato chips at the bus station in Ecuador after finding the length of the bus ride expanded from four hours to eight hours; other than that, I have never eaten street food.

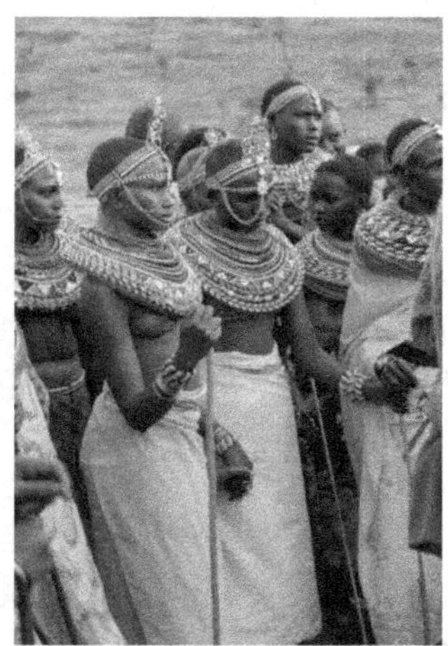

*9. Wedding festival, Kenya*

### *EATING ALONE*

Eating alone offers a splendid opportunity for a number of reasons. People-watching tops my list. Observing the habits and customs of another culture leads to intriguing revelations in a restaurant. You might have the opportunity to strike up a conversation with someone and make a new friend. Chat with the waiter about his/her favorite recommendations even though you do not speak the language. Figure out a way to communicate with them. What better time than this to reflect on your day's experiences and jot notes or make journal entries. I never sit in a restaurant without my notebook and pen.

Many people prefer to travel alone with the exception of going to eat alone. Most do not look forward to sitting alone, meal after meal. Sometimes you get a table by the kitchen door or at the back of the room in a dark corner. Ask for a new location or go to another restaurant. Ask for a good table, speak with the manager if possible when making reservations, and explain your solo dining status.

Consider buying local foods at the market like bread, cheese, fruit, vegetables, and eat in your room or order room service if the hotel offers it. Better yet, buy some pastries and fruit, relax in the city square (every town has one), and watch locals interacting with each other.

Peace Corps has a saying to remember when traveling to undeveloped countries, "Boil it, cook it, peel it, or forget it." Translated, the above statement means all fresh fruits and vegetables need boiling or peeling before you consume them.

### *REMOTE SITUATIONS*

Leaving tourist-traveled areas behind means you will have a limited ability to find places selling safe food. Have local currency if possible. You can sometimes find a family with extra food or a market. When off the beaten track, hire a young person as a guide. For little money, they can save your life, time after time. Knowing the area, they can predict how much food to take or where you might buy fruits and vegetables along the way. Depending on your diet and how much you like to eat, you might want to take canned meats, beef jerky, nuts, coffee and power bars. The local grain may show up as porridge or pancakes but expect difficulty in finding inexpensive protein. Small packets of peanut butter and cheese, mini cans of tuna or chicken, and beef jerky pack well.

Local markets open your eyes to the vast diversity between cultures. Trails weave in and out for blocks in some markets like Bangkok, Addis Ababa, and Bamako. Big markets, like those in Singapore and Jakarta, have distinct areas, divided into crafts, clothing, and food. Peel any vegetables or fruits you buy before you eat them, soak them in a sink with ten drops of iodine, or bleach for 20 minutes. Avoid ice cubes. Order all bottled drinks unopened and without ice. Many occasions I have ordered a soda or bottled water and had it served at my table in a glass full of ice. Ice may come from the local bacteria-containing water. For emergencies, keep extra food on hand. You never know when you will arrive in a town where the sanitary conditions suggest you stay away from cafes. Never leave on a bus without food for the trip. Buses break down. Food stops offer no solutions and may even look repulsive. Sardines, if you can stand them, appear available just about every place I have ever traveled.

When in Ethiopia, I took all my own food for three weeks. We traveled in dry riverbeds, and we could not see any markets. I found homemade bread in every village, and almost every day I found eggs for sale. I carried individual packets of oatmeal and mixed in protein powder for breakfast. The same treatment works with hot chocolate, soup mixes, and any of the incredible variety of dehydrated foods in packets at camping or travel stores and catalogs. Sources of protein include protein bars, "no carbohydrate" bars, cheese sticks, nuts, all types of foil-wrapped or canned meats, and beef jerky.

You have to develop a taste for eating the same kinds of foods every day. Before you leave on your trip, give yourself a couple of weeks to adjust. Make a protein bar your lunch a few times. Try the oatmeal because if you cannot stomach it at home, you will suffer on your trip. Traveling takes a lot of energy, and food feeds your mental and physical well-being. The people in remote areas often eat one meal a day, such as one sweet potato or one gourd of millet porridge. Plan, search different catalogs for ideas, and try the food before you leave. In your research, find out if building fires is allowed. The desert offers no firewood. The Tuareg people taught me how to burn camel dung.

Pack small and nesting items when organizing your gear for cooking. One tiny pot for boiling instant meals or water, one plate, one cup, a fork, and a spoon filled my cooking requirements in Ethiopia. I have never carried stoves because I never wanted the hassles of fuel. Some campers prefer tiny compacts like those international stoves offered at campmor.com, starting at less than fifty dollars. Tea bags, or the coffee that comes in bags like tea, can help. Boil your drinking water for safety unless you have a water purifier. Take your own herbal tea, as I have never seen decaffeinated products in underdeveloped countries. Explore creativity. Leave room for fruit bars with 100% natural fruit, available at natural food stores. These offer you special treats to anticipate. On the internet, find all kinds of travel containers of packets, like peanut butter and real maple syrup for those sorghum pancakes that taste so bland.

### *WATER*

Inadequate access to drinkable water affects almost 900 million people worldwide. Avoid the practice of brushing your teeth and drinking water when traveling to undeveloped countries. Bottled water offers an inexpensive and available solution, even in the most unusual places, and hot water exists if the village has electricity or a generator. Check with the Center for Disease Control and Prevention (CDC) before traveling. A trip to an undeveloped or Second World country does not suggest contaminated water. In South Africa, you can drink the city tap water, but in Costa Rica, you cannot. According to the CDC, travelers face high risk in Mexico, Central America, most of Africa, Asia, and the Middle East.

I am obsessed with staying healthy when I travel. I used to carry a water purifier everywhere, used it for years in muddy rivers, and escaped sickness. The SteriPen works well if you can find clear river water or tap water. If not, the sediment will need to settle to the bottom of the container before use. The SteriPen is tiny and compact, but it's high–priced; I think it is worth every penny.

After hiking for several days in the jungles of Borneo, I will never forget the greeting I received in a ten-hut village. The chief walked up to me with a huge porcelain bowl, half-full of river water, with two Fanta orange sodas in bottles. I never could figure out how he got those glass bottles so far from the city without breaking them.

### *HOTELS*

Everyone must deal with finding shelter. If I could find a recommended hotel and reserve it for my initial arrival and pre-departure days in an area, I would have a safe and dependable solution to my need for shelter. European-style hotels, hostels, and pensiones have various costs and features. Unless you have the money, have a fear of becoming acquainted with the local lifestyle, or cannot leave luxury behind, then small neighborhood hotels could save you money. Living where the locals hang out provides a sense of the locale. Unlike the United States, foreign hotels expect walk-ins without reservations, due to their slower pace. In larger cities, if they have a phone, or if you know their e-mail address, you can book a reservation before you arrive for your first night. Many hotels and guesthouses have e-mail addresses now listed in guidebooks and online. Arriving in a foreign city, you encounter officials wanting your documents and your cab fare, all in a foreign language. Reserving a room adds comfort to your first night.

In my opinion, for smaller towns, guidebooks have value for finding a room. They will list rooms according to price, and they will list amenities as well as possible detractions. Facilities available, cleanliness, Wi-Fi, private bathrooms, friendliness of managers vary with every listing. I double what the guidebook suggests, and often my figure for cost comes closer to the actual price. Owners of hotels, hostels, pensiones, campements, and even grass huts lust for the opportunity to see their name in a guidebook.

Read several authors for guidebooks and copy the chapters that include your destination and take it with you. When you find a hotel, ask to see the room before you pay, even including a hammock under a tin roof. If unacceptable, ask for a discount or ask to see another room.

Make sure the doors and windows lock, the place looks clean, and the air conditioner, hot water, or heater work if you paid for it. Ask for clean sheets and towels if these items are not in the room. You pay for what you get. "Bathroom" means "bathing facilities" in Europe, and these rooms do not include a toilet. If you want a toilet in your room, you will pay a higher cost.

Avoid rooms with a lot of street noise or in an unsafe location. If you arrive in a town not included in your guidebook, or if you have an unplanned stopover somewhere, ask other travelers you see getting off the plane or bus for their recommendations. Before making a decision in this case, I try to visit two or three places and then make a choice. Beware as taxi drivers are known for telling you the hotel of your choice is full or closed just to make a commission from taking you to their choice of hotels that pay them a nice fee. If making a reservation on an online bidding or auction site, beware. Many hotels call a king bed a standard room. Bidding on sites like Priceline.com means you don't have the ability to change the terms of the winning bid until you arrive. If you bid on a standard room, but on arrival all they have are the king beds you booked, you will not be allowed to change. Use your imagination and spend time researching ideas like staying in a castle, villa in the country, a parador in Spain, a pousada in Portugal, a treetop hotel in Paris or Brazil, a prison in England, an ice hotel in Sweden, a Bedouin tent camp in Jordan, a church in Scotland, a glass igloo in

Finland, a concrete sewer pipe in Austria, a four-star cave in Italy, a windmill in Greece, a yurt in Spain, or an undersea hotel in the United States.

Use your imagination and do your homework as you check out: www.travel.cnn.com/explorations/escape/15-unusual-places-spend-night-213174, www.unusualhotelsoftheworld.com, and also look into sites such as www.cottagetocastles.com, www.paradorsofspain.com, www.pousada.com.

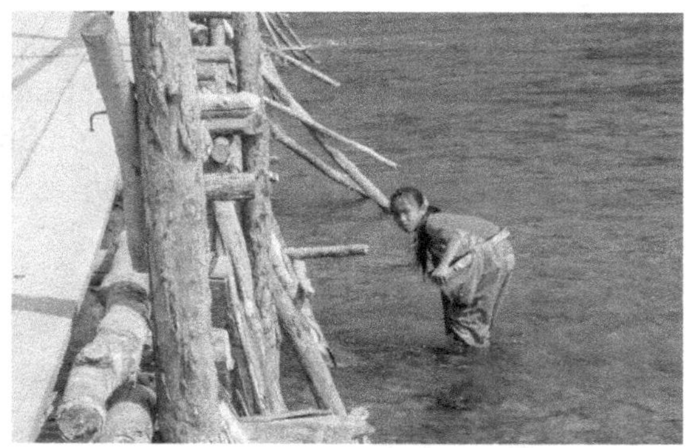

*10. Girl fishing in Vientiane, Laos*

### *HOME EXCHANGES*

Home exchanging changes the way people travel. Checking profiles of homes in a country you are not familiar with piques your curiosity about another culture.

Live like the locals and save on accommodations. Choose a townhouse in New York or a hacienda in Spain or any shape/size of house found around the globe. www.1sthomeexchange.com; www.homeexhange.com; or www.rick-steves.com/plan/tis/0400swap.htm,

### *HOSTELS*

Hostels used to cater to young backpacking people. Now hostels, although organized through the International Youth Hostel Federation, can offer accommodations for any age with a discount for those over fifty-nine. Hostels have set rules, which vary according to location. Communal meals may exist, or they might offer a kitchen well equipped with cooking and eating utensils. You cook for yourself and clean up. Community meals at a budget hotel in Kunming, China, meant everyone ate out of the same bowl with their own chopsticks. Most of the guests around me had coughs. I had saved two dollars by joining in the community dinner, but I ended up in contact with my fellow travelers' viruses. Hostels may or may not represent safe, clean, and perfect places to meet other travelers. People from all parts of the world stay in hostels. The hours of operation vary. The doors lock at night, beginning between 10:00 PM and 12:00 AM, and some close during the day.

You leave all your belongings in a locker or by your bed, dormitory style, and return late afternoon. Check with the hostel to find out the rules.

Many hostels are relaxed now with rules including no membership required in any hostel organization. Large, shared rooms separate men and women. A few hostels have family and couples' rooms. Hostels may limit your stay to a few days. Use caution when booking online or checking in when you don't speak the language.

### *YMCAs*

Throughout the world, you will find either YMCAs or YWCAs. At some, you can reserve rooms, and some require a small membership fee. In Singapore, they asked for a one-time ten-dollar membership fee. Their rates cost more in comparison to other budget places in the guidebooks. They offered a wealth of information and bus passes. Many families with children stayed there.

### *OTHER TYPES OF SHELTER*

Sleeping on an overnight train or bus can save on hotel expenses. However, you may not sleep without interruption from the stops, noises, and anxiety of keeping your gear safe. Transportation in any foreign country requires close watch of your luggage. When the bus stops to unload passengers, make sure your bag stays. Traveling during the day provides an opportunity to see the country, pass farmers in fields, view small villages bustling with activity, and observe schoolchildren playing in schoolyards. Many overnight boat trips in Asia and South America require, as part of your gear, a hammock. You can find inexpensive hammocks in towns where boats dock. Tents or mosquito nets serve as a necessary protection in countries with malarial risks. Guidebooks will suggest their use. Determine how far off the beaten track your trip will take you. If you stay on the pancake trail (the well-traveled road where you can meet other travelers like yourself, even in the most remote places), you can buy equipment from other travelers heading home or from the local shops. Some locals may have mosquito nets to share, helping you avoid exposure to malaria.

# Chapter 8: documents

*"A mind that is stretched by a new experience can never go back to its old dimensions."* Oliver Wendell Holmes

***PASSPORTS***

Travel outside the United States requires a passport. The new laws require a passport when leaving the borders of the United States. Cruising to nearby islands requires either a passport or passport identification card. Use your passport for identification when renting cars, etc. Use selected libraries, post offices, clerks of court, municipal government offices or private passport agencies to apply for a passport. When applying for a passport, you will need proof of U.S. citizenship, such as a previous passport or a certified birth certificate. You must have two identical and recent photographs. Your picture should be taken front view, full face, on a light background and should be two by two inches. Your face should measure one to one and one-half inches.

You will also need a valid US identity such as a driver's license or corporate ID card, intent to travel for expedited services, and money for a ten-year passport. Look for passport services online, which will expedite the process. The US Passport Bureau will expedite the process for extra money, but you need proof of intent to travel soon like a flight reservation or request for foreign visa. Online and private agencies will expedite the process for fees starting at around $150 for a one-week turnaround, but they require you to appear before a certified office (like those listed above) to verify your identity. Passports cost $100 but, as of this writing, will go up to $135 to help pay for the additional passport centers opened recently. For mail applications, get a DSP-82, "Application for Passport by Mail," from the post office or courts. Mail application rules require that you had a previous passport issued within the last twelve years. Include your previous passport, two identical photographs, and money. Your old passport will be returned to you with a hole punched in the cover. I saved three old ones. My first passport traveled around the world twice. Opening my old passport recalls dreams fulfilled.

Request a forty-eight-page passport or write for extra visa pages for frequent travel. This used to be free, but now costs eighty-two dollars. If you change your name due to a court order or marriage, you can receive a free name change added to the last page of your passport if it is less than a year old. Check www.travel.state.gov for current information, forms, and necessary documents. For passports over a year old, follow the procedure for the above, and include the current renewal fees.

### *VISAS*

Some countries require a visa or official stamp in your passport for entry. Check online to find out. Just Google, "Do I need a visa for Bangkok?" Various sites will offer the answer. Obtain a visa stamp in your passport before leaving the United States, placed there by a foreign government that allows you to travel within that country for a specific period. You can obtain visas abroad but not for all countries. Besides, if you take care of this before you leave the United States, the processing time will not eat into your travel time. Your plans may change, and you will have no alternative other than to get a visa abroad. Write to the consulate or embassy for each country you intend to visit, and allow for processing and delays. I have had several time-consuming experiences with obtaining visas.

The person answering your call for information will volunteer to mail or FAX an application, or you can go online to download applications. Several embassies request you send everything to them by Fed Ex or UPS, thus adding cost. Follow all instructions and rules. Ask for EVERYTHING they require for obtaining a visa to their country. Ask all the specific questions you can think of, keeping in mind the person you talk to will not speak English well. Always ask again, and get assurance that this completes ALL that you need to send. Ask even if the question sounds crazy. Some common questions: How much money is required? What form of payment (cashier's check or money order) is acceptable? Is a photograph necessary? How many? Is your health certificate required for any reason? Are you required to supply the dates of your travel and itinerary? Must you state the purpose of your trip? How long will it take you get the visa? Check if the electronic visa issued in advance, or visa on entry, applies to seaports as well as airports. India may be a country where a cruise passenger might be refused entry or even embarkation access to an expensive cruise if the expected visa is not available at the seaport.

If they ask your occupation, journalists and photographers, beware. Many Fourth World countries frown on these occupations. They may not let you enter.

After completing the application and compiling all of the required documents, call the agency again to verify you have filled out and supplied them with everything they require. You may find in your follow-up call that you have reached a different person. From this person, you may find out that now they require a letter from your doctor specifying you have tested negative for AIDS. You never know what can change between the time they send the forms and the day you fill them out.

Call them on the day they said they would return your visa. Your request may sit on someone's desk unopened. Call again in a few days to check. I would start all these proceedings as far in advance as possible, at least a month or more before your departure.

My application for a visa to one African country took over two months of repeated mailings. Two days before my departure, I thought I would need to change my outbound flight to include a stopover in Chicago so I could walk in and get my passport with the visa stamped inside. One last phone call from me, though, and they realized I needed to leave in two days; they sent the passport to me via Fed Ex overnight delivery--at my cost, of course.

People from other countries often approach business transactions in different ways. If you have frustration with visa applications, remember this indicates what may lie ahead.

Visas have specific periods for use and, unless specified, limit you to a one-time use. Go to www.travel.state.gov/visa to find out if a visa is required in the country of your destination. Search online to find out if you can get your visa at a stopover on the way, which might take a few days but save you much money. Check travel blogs and forums to find out if there are time-saving steps in obtaining a visa. Remain courteous and respectful when communicating with the embassy or consular office. They can help in answering questions, too.

Wanting to travel to Burma, I knew I did not have time to obtain the expensive visa in the United States; plus, it would take a couple of months. On a travel forum, someone said if you book a small tour with a travel agent in Burma, they will have your visa waiting at the airport. I emailed an agency all my information and a copy of a photo and, sure enough, the visa was ready when I arrived, and I only paid about twenty dollars for it. The agent charged me five dollars for his time.

While traveling back and forth between Cambodia and Vietnam, I received a visa at the airport upon arrival in Cambodia. After two weeks in Cambodia, I traveled via the river into Vietnam, stopping at the border crossing to have my visa stamped "exit" for Cambodia. I purchased a single-entry visa for Vietnam while in Cambodia for thirty dollars. I had no problem entering Vietnam from Cambodia via the Vinh Xuong border on a six-hour boat ride, costing less than ten dollars.

My last nights in Chau Doc, Vietnam, included encounters with unsociable locals until I met a young English-speaking teacher at a local school who invited me to help with English classes. He knew that I had a sour taste in my mouth for Chau Doc, so he had a small hand-carved canoe meet me the next morning for a visit to several local villages. Pottery makers, weavers, and farmers met me with welcoming smiles and invitations to meet their families. The teacher invited me to ride to the border with his group, and we shared information from my guidebook the entire trip. The *Lonely Planet* guidebook has history, geography, flora, fauna and all kinds of interesting tidbits the teacher had never read about. He left me at the Vietnam border and returned to Chau Doc. I could not cross the Cambodia border as my single-entry visa had an exit stamp. I had not thought ahead about needing a multiple-entry visa.

The Vietnamese border patrol refused to allow me to travel back into Vietnam as they had just stamped my single-entry visa with "exit." On the beach between two countries, with no place to go, I went back and forth between patrol officers. I begged them to help me, and I even offered two hundred dollars to encourage them. The Vietnamese officers handed me a form to sign that was several pages long in their language. I refused, explaining as best I could that I was not going to sign papers I could not understand. About two hours later, my new Vietnamese friend, the teacher I had only just met within the last couple of days, came back on his boat. He explained to me that someone called him on his radio to tell him about my situation. They told him that his English friend had serious trouble. He promised the border officers that he would take me to Ho Chi Minh City (HCMC) to get things straightened out with the American embassy. I had given my friend my thirty-dollar guidebook for Vietnam, thinking he could use it for his English class. The old saying, "What you give you will get back ten-fold" came true plus more. I could not put a price on my friend's rescue of me, helping to find a local bus for Saigon, and salvaging my trip. You might not be so lucky to find such a friend abroad, so pay the extra twenty dollars or so for a multiple-entry visa. You never know if you will get the chance to leave and return to the same country, and you should always be prepared.

### TOURIST CARDS

A few countries require an additional tourist card to cross their borders. Get the card from the country's embassy or consulate. The airline may pass them out before you land.

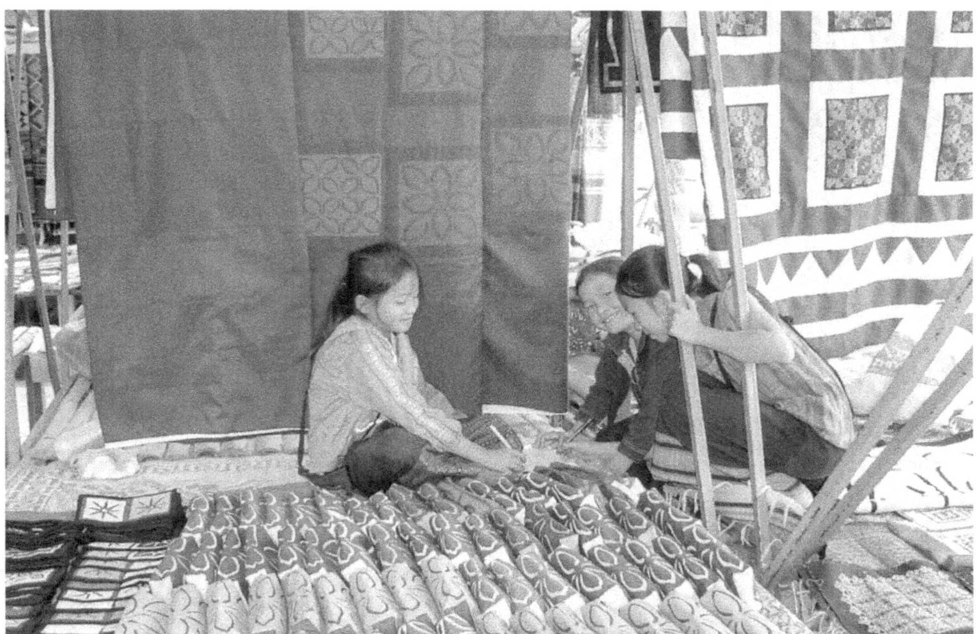

11. Girls selling fabric, Laos market

### IMMUNIZATIONS AND MEDICAL RECORDS

Take with you your yellow International Vaccinations Certificate and all other medical records needed in case of medical emergencies abroad.

If you have pre-existing conditions, get a letter from your doctor describing your situation, mentioning all prescribed medicines. This simplifies passing through customs. Leave all drugs in their original labeled containers. Educate yourself about your prescription's generic names before you leave. If you have allergies or reactions to drugs, you should consider wearing a medical alert bracelet.

Go to www.nc.cdc.gov/travel to find out which vaccines are required for the country of your destination.

### *INSURANCE*

Take all identity cards and claim forms with you, but do not count on your local insurance company accepting claims from international countries.

### *DRIVER'S LICENSE*

Take your driver's license. You may need to rent a car. Check with the embassy or consular office of your destination country for information on requirements for an international driver's license. AAA provides that service in the US. Some countries may not require an international driver's license.

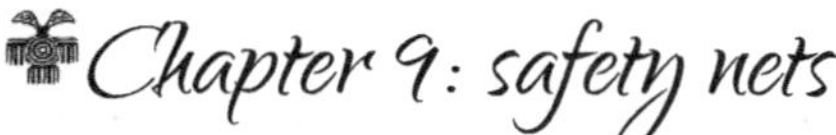

# Chapter 9: safety nets

*"The world doesn't end when you decide to do what you want to do. It merely begins."* Ed Buryn

***TRAVEL SAFELY***

Travelers seldom think of the pitfalls, hazards, and other risky business as anything they might encounter after leaving home. Traveling in faraway surroundings, hearing new languages, pulling or carrying heavy bags, and wearing waist packs, sagging with money, can make you a prime target for thieves, beggars, and young entrepreneurs wanting to take advantage. You cannot hide from those wanting to separate you from your money. Crime happens. Travelers risk theft, rape, and accidents. However, preventive calculations and measures can reduce the inherent travel exposures.

When we leave the comforts of home, our vulnerability increases. Our routines take us down familiar paths, almost as if we are hypnotized, pulling into the same parking space day after day, etc. Lost in fantasies, we ignore most of what goes on around us. Being caught up in daydreams or to-do lists lowers our defenses. As we grow, we build barriers to protect us from accidents and crime. We do not think about these automatic barriers. Fastening seatbelts, locking doors, pulling blinds, asking for escorts to rental cars in lots late at night, and maintaining memberships in emergency road service plans make sense. These relate to the mechanical habits of normal life. Many of the capabilities, resources, and techniques it takes to make your trip a safe one you already have. However, when you travel abroad, you will need to initiate others. Stay observant and alert to your new surroundings to ensure a higher level of safety.

Simple precautions can ease the burden of safety while traveling in unfamiliar territory. After learning what dangers to expect, and how to handle them, you will lighten your emotional load. Remember, fear arises from the unknown. Information and self-education for the adventure ahead helps you to prepare and defend yourself. Preparation for minimizing dangers begins at home. While making travel arrangements, you must make decisions. Decide where to go, what to pack, what you will do, and consider the what-ifs.

A concern for safety helps to make the trip pleasant, and finding the answers to your questions before you leave will minimize your risk. In making travel plans to New Guinea, I researched every source I could find for facts about the tribes and made extensive notes on those considered unreliable or hostile. Notes on recommended trails, or those classified as slippery, steep, or dangerous give one a basis for an itinerary when talking with a guide.

Check out: www.travel.state.gov/travel/tips/safety

For safety ideas, try: www.safetravel.dot.gov

For emergency tips: www.travel.state.gov/travel/tips/emergencies

***EXTRA FORESIGHT***

Do extra planning when traveling in less industrialized countries. Carry extra copies of the personal information page of your passport with you at all times in a separate location other than in your passport. Keep one in your luggage and one at home for a friend to find in case of emergencies. Do the same with the 800 numbers of your credit cards, and make sure you write down the card number in a safe place. If you e-mail these numbers to yourself, you will have a backup option to print off.

While walking downtown in Addis Ababa, I met up with a group of young men.

One asked if he could try on my hiking boots. He said he didn't want to buy them but just try them on. Can you guess what would have happened if I had let him? My guidebook had warned of meeting with street boys like these. I laughed and waved them on, and I still wonder what they thought I would wear if I gave them my boots. Anticipate situations not encountered in your home country. Flash floods, volcanoes, and washed-out snaky roads strewn with fallen rock can wreak havoc during your adventure.

Guidebooks will warn you of poisonous plants, creepy critters, and wild animals, still roaming in obscure parts of the world. Before you leave, find out which regions have such hazards.

At the top of an incline, my Ethiopian driver and I faced a roaring forest fire heading fast in our direction. The narrow steep embankment meant backing up, but the deep sand played games with our four-wheel drive. About a mile down the riverbed road, I realized we had no radio or method to learn how to find an alternative route. We lost two days of driving time by not having optional routes planned and having to go to a small city to find help and a better map.

Never leave drinks or open bottles alone on a table or counter while you use the phone or toilet. Rohypnol, also called the date rape drug, causes a sedative affect and leaves you open to robbery and rape. Never accept drinks from strangers or even someone you only know slightly. Otherwise, you might find yourself kidnapped or dumped in a ditch after being robbed.

### *FLYING*

During airline selection, note the differences in safety factors in other countries. In the United States Government Travel Advisories, sometimes you will find that a country's internal airline may not meet FAA standards. Leaving a small town in Borneo, I trembled as my plane left the ground. Rain dripped down the cabin walls. The captain's glasses looked like Coke bottles. I wondered how he could see the newspaper he read while, at the same time, flying our plane. Every few minutes he would stop to shake the ashes from his cigar.

### *PETS*

Research online for safety tips, hotel regulations, and the requirements for transporting pets on public buses, trains, or planes. Options for commercial plane travel have changed dramatically over the years to include expensive fees. Fees vary depending on whether the pet flies inside the cabin under a seat or is transported as cargo (requiring extra time and handling). For airline travel, always book your flights early as airlines limit the number of pets inside the cabins.

Choose the best carrier for your animal, making sure the door is secure. Your pet should be able to stand up, turn around, and lie down in comfort. Each airline has its own rules about the size of pet carriers for various planes. A call should be made to the airlines before travel since maximum size requirements of pet carriers can be determined by the flight.

Several weeks before travel, pet owners should acclimate their pets to their carriers. Allow your pet to ride in the carrier on the floor of your car so it can feel the vibration. Attach your name, address, and phone number to the carrier, along with the destination address and phone number. Do the same for your pet's collar.

Within ten days of departure, take your pet for a vet checkup. Get a health certificate because this will be required at various stops during travel. Trim your animal's nails so they will not be caught in cracks and doors. Bring a leash for your dog and give it an extra-long walk before travel time to tire it out. He will do better traveling if he does it while sleeping. Do not leave the leash inside the carrier as the pet might get tangled in it. If attached to the outside, the leash might get caught in the conveyor belt while loading in the plane.

Do not feed your pet for four to six hours before travel. Have a photograph of your pet in case it becomes separated from you. After arrival at your destination, take your pet to a safe place, open the carrier, and check your pet to make sure it is doing all right.

The incidents of lost, injured, and dead pets have risen due to the hundreds of thousands of pets traveling by plane each year.

Airlines restrict pet travel when temperatures are expected to exceed eighty-five degrees or go below twenty degrees at an airport. Persian cats and snub-nosed dogs like bulldogs are not allowed as cargo on many airlines since they are prone to breathing problems.

Some airlines ban these breeds from all planes. Choose direct non-peak flights. Changing planes usually does not allow for walking a pet or taking it for a toilet break.

Crowded planes can also stress your pet. Climate-controlled holding areas and frequent-flier programs are some of the pet-friendly rewards airlines are offering now.

Always travel on the same flight as your pet. Some owners are giving pets their own vacation at kennels near airports. The more expensive kennels offer TVs with animal shows, ventilation systems (so pets cannot smell other animals), and extra cuddling.

### *SMOKING*

Smoking is not permitted on airlines. This includes smokeless cigarettes and e-cigarettes. Expensive penalties exist for tampering with smoke detectors inside plane toilet areas, so do not think you can sneak into the bathroom to smoke.

Plan to pack your favorite brands, and plenty of them, in case you are unable to find cigarettes where you are heading. In remote Ethiopia, I met a man shaking and pacing the road.

I asked him if my guide or I could help. He said he ran out of cigarettes and the small markets did not sell them.

### *CHOOSE A SAFE HOTEL*

Your hotel should feel like your home away from home. Is your hotel in a safe location? Can you walk at night to shops and restaurants? Does it have a safe where you can store items to avoid them being stolen from your room? Hotels do not carry insurance for lost or stolen items in rooms, so make sure your hotel offers a safe.

Good hotels have well-lighted or gated parking lots. Remember, theft creates unnecessary hassles. Swimming pools and exercise rooms often have no supervision. Do not go swimming in the hotel pool late at night alone. You put yourself in danger.

Avoid taking a room at the end of a long corridor. This can leave you trapped, should someone follow you into the hotel. Ask for a room above the first floor to keep peeping toms away and to reduce the risk of someone breaking in through your window. Change rooms if sliding glass doors have no locks. Eliminate the opportunity for strangers to find out your room number. Have packages delivered to the front desk, rather than to your room. Develop a habit of keeping a flashlight close by after dark.

Although you may not face a disaster in the middle of the night, have a plan to leave, or at least check the situation out after dark with a flashlight so you are at least familiar with the territory. Keep your glasses, flashlight, room key, and money belt on the same side of your bed every night, so you are not fumbling in the dark if you need to get out of your room quickly. Hearing a fire alarm at 1:00 a.m. can startle anyone. Running out of a room without your essentials could ruin your trip.

For years, I have used a small net bag for my flashlight, glass case, and luggage keys. That bag stays beside my head on the right side of my bed when I sleep, and my money pouch is always tucked away safely under my pillow. A mouse tiptoeing on my shoulder, a spider on my face, a tree limb brushing the tent, or someone creeping into my room will all cause me to jump for my little bag.

Remain alert when in a strange location without protection. Make sure you know where all the fire escapes are located so you can get to safety in the case of a fire. But remember, if you're traveling alone, the fire escape might threaten your safety. If your room is next to one, and your room has large windows or sliding doors that do not lock tight, a thief or rapist could sneak up the fire escape and get into your room.

Take your hotel's business card when you walk out the hotel door. A name means nothing to the taxi driver who speaks and reads another language. Many have little maps on the backside of their cards, so you can walk back without hassles. Wandering a new town and seeing a foreign sign helps to confuse the traveler, plus, the smaller the city, the less chance of finding or reading street signs. Ask the clerk at your hotel to write the hotel name and street (or directions) in the local language in your handy notebook. Write the name and city in English underneath that, in case someday you want to return to the same place. After five trips to Bangkok, I convinced myself to do that. I knew the location of the hotel I liked staying in, and I could point the driver to the exact alleyway close by it, but I never knew the name of the establishment until I asked.

### *PREVENTING THEFT*

A little preparation before and during your trip will help keep you and your valuables safe. Think about the probability of robbery or theft. Try to manage your wardrobe, jewelry, valuables, and documents so that whatever you lose does not hinder your adventure. Keep critical essentials on your person. Then consider the rest of your belongings as replaceable.

Small cable ties work great to deter a thief, as they cannot be broken with the hands but need to be cut. If your luggage is broken into by airline employees, airport security personnel, taxi drivers, or anyone entering your hotel room while you are away, the cut cable tie will let you know. Otherwise you might not miss something until it is too late to report to the proper authorities.

### *MONEY SCAMS*

Even the best travelers have trouble with money scams. The results of the best scam feel like a game of magic performed for your private viewing. You give the moneychanger a new hundred-dollar bill. He counts out the converted amount in front of you, and hands it to you to count. He will use small bills, which take longer to count. You count the bills, verifying he has given you the correct amount. He reaches for the cash in your hand, pretending to count again himself. Somehow, he slips that stack under the table, and places another stack on the table before you realize what he's done. That stack is short by twenty dollars or more. He pretends to count again, moving very fast so you don't notice the shortage. You will find variations on how you can be shorted.

Seek out a bank or other reputable source for exchanging cash and for all your money dealings in a foreign country.

### *JEWELRY*

Avoid taking valuables like jewelry, expensive clothes, and the laptop computer in your favorite leather briefcase. Jewelry attracts attention. When I travel, I wear things that have no monetary or sentimental value. Women have different feelings about wearing wedding rings or just a simple band. Some women I have met love the freedom of travel, and they notice that without a ring, they meet more intriguing people, engage in extraordinary conversations, and develop lifelong friendships or relationships. The conservative woman believes a wedding band protects her from a stranger's advances. Compromise and take off your wedding band when appropriate, but remember where you put it. In any event, never wear sparkling diamonds.

### *PEPPER SPRAY*

Purchase pepper spray for your waist pouch or belt, if appropriate. Traveling alone, catching trains at midnight, trekking into out-of-the way places, walking on unlit paths, and staying in bargain rooms require added security. Often when I walk into a questionable situation, like a busy market or packed train station, I keep a finger on the button of the spray. This warning helps to repel potential thieves. For peace of mind, I avoid groups of men or older boys. Laws in some American states forbid the purchase of pepper spray. You can buy yours in foreign markets. Traveling on foreign planes, I carry my pepper spray deep in my camera case when going through customs and security.

### *AIRPORT SCANNERS*

Airport scanners leave you defenseless. Thieves work in pairs—one will create a distraction, or engage you in conversation, while the other grabs your valuables before you know what happened. Put your briefcase, laptop, and money belt into the scanner last so you stay close to them. If possible, hide your money belt inside a carry-on, or wear it under your shirt, minimizing the risk that it will be seen. Keep your eyes on your belongings even during an airport search. Count the number of items placed on the belt. Sometimes, if you have many items, you can lose track of your jacket or other valuables. Stories abound on this subject as you meet fellow travelers and they talk about valuables stolen from scanner belts.

An airline hostess noticed my tears while taking off on a flight out of Texas. I told her someone stole my jade ring from the dish going through the scanner, and I did not notice until I boarded. I grabbed all my jewelry, and instead of putting on the ring, I just dumped it into a side pocket with all my other jewelry. She called the captain and had him radio TSA to look for the ring. During the first stopover, the captain shared countless stories with me about this very type of thing, and he advised me to remove my jewelry before getting to a security checkpoint, to put it in a safe place, and to avoid using the dish provided. I did get the ring back, three months later.

Some Third and Fourth World airports have difficult layouts for security. You may find yourself separated from your carry-ons and put into another room or behind a curtain for a full body search. This provides opportunities for someone to remove items from your carry-ons. Airline officials contribute to the problem. I say this from first-hand observation. Prior to leaving Addis Ababa on Alitalia Airlines, I walked out of the curtained area to find my bags open, with half the contents gone. I could not find anyone around. I wrote to Alitalia to complain, and they took no responsibility. They said the employees worked for Ethiopian Airlines. I wrote Ethiopian Airlines, and they responded that the employees worked for the airport, not the airline. They accepted no responsibility even though the employees wore Ethiopian Airline uniforms and badges.

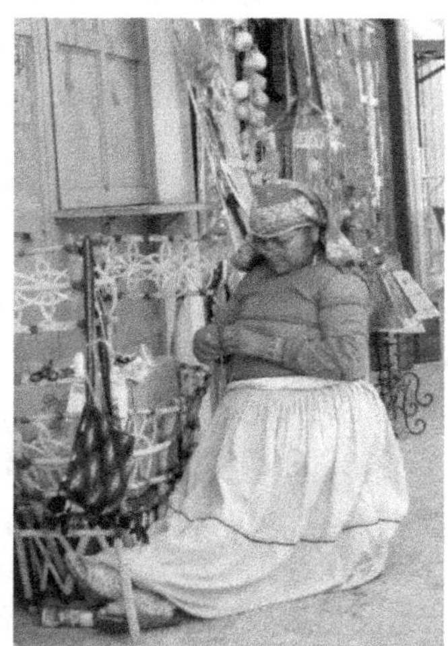

*12. Woman making basket, Mexico*

Now I put a small lock on all my bags, including carry-ons. I put all waist packs, purses, cell phones, and other single items inside the carry-on and lock it tightly.

Holidays and peak times create additional concern. Large crowds and long waiting lines lead to frustrating experiences. Arrange to buy tickets in advance and arrive well before the scheduled check-in time in order to establish your place at the beginning of the line. Those first in line receive a bit of seniority. In remote airports, locals have pushed in front of me without tickets or reservations. My name on a reserved list meant nothing.

In Coca, a small jungle town in the Amazon, I waited in line for two days for my reserved flight departure. The airline ignored the reserved list and said I could not board. Locals walked past me and got boarding passes. The third day I screamed at the manager and held tight to the ticket counter, not allowing anyone to get in front of me. They issued me a boarding pass, acting as if they had never seen me before.

### *LUGGAGE*

The remoteness of your trip, the distance, and the number of plane changes will increase the possibility of damage to your belongings or theft of your property. Tag luggage inside and out and make sure the luggage has locks.

You can purchase wire clips from travel product catalogs, suitable for one-time use. If you find these broken during a trip, you know someone has opened your luggage.

In Third and Fourth World countries, planes may sit for a day, which means your luggage might sit out in the open with no security.

Luggage must have information attached to it with your contact information. If you check in your luggage, make sure your baggage claim check has the correct destination. Newer luggage tags have hidden address information, thus minimizing the possibility of thieves targeting your home while you are out of town.

Carrying a small wire cable with looped ends and a padlock offers another security measure. Loop this through ALL your luggage handles or straps, and then around a stationary object. This easy preventive keeps thieves from grabbing and running off with one of your bags.

On a bus or train, the wire-cable lock can be wrapped around the leg of your seat while you are sleeping. In a hotel or grass hut with nothing attached to the floor, I loop the wire through everything in sight, securing the bags during my absence each day. At least this deters the "grab a bag and run" thief. Cables exist for sale at any camping or travel outlet, or make your own.

Never leave your luggage in a transportation terminal, even if you must use the restroom. Count your bags every time you get on or off a bus or train.

### *RENTAL CARS*

Privacy and the ability to go where you want to go far outweigh the disadvantages of rental cars. Use common sense, and remember the road rules of the country. Make sure you drive on the correct side of the road. When you leave the rental-car agency or hotel, have a map showing you how to return. Ask the rental clerk for clear directions on how to get to your destination and the dangerous neighborhoods to avoid. Park in well-lighted parking lots, and hide everything in your trunk including maps. Maps can identify you as a tourist. In Puerto Rico, I rented a car after dark and did not notice all of the dents around the bumpers until the next day. Though I was now six hours from the rental agency, I called to report the dents. This solved a potential problem in returning the vehicle.

### *TAXIS*

If you should hail a taxi, but then feel uncomfortable with the driver for whatever reason, do not get in the vehicle. If you feel impolite and this makes you feel you must go against your instincts, don't give in to that. Say you have to go and make a phone call, or make another excuse and walk away.

You depend on the driver to take you where you need to go. In Third World cities, I have never had a problem with taxi drivers. They often lose their way, trying to find my little out-of-the-way inns, but somehow, they manage to find them. They might have to stop several times for directions from other locals, but they get me where I need to be. All that being said, know where the driver takes you, and have a general idea of how long the trip should take. Try to have a map, a business card from the hotel, and instructions on how to get to your destination.

Once in New York City, I had a hundred-dollar bill, owed the driver ten dollars, and needed to get home. The driver said he had no change. I put one foot on the ground and yelled for help. "Police!" People passed by without flinching, and nobody came to my rescue. I had no alternative but to let him leave with the money I had saved to use to return home.

Thieves hop in taxis at traffic lights. When in Rio de Janeiro, I heard a common practice of thieves included throwing a poisonous snake into a taxi. The frightened driver would hop out, and the thief would pull the snake out with a stick and drive off. Taking taxis requires always looking out for yourself. Be on guard for any kind of situation. In Kenya, a common practice was to rob tourists in taxis at stop lights.

### *HIDING MONEY OR DOCUMENTS*

During the day, while away from my sleeping quarters, I carry all documents in a thin waist pouch that has a belt. I wear this under all my clothing. Everything rests in one plastic bag to prevent sweat from ruining the documents. On the outside of my clothing, I wear a pouch with zipper openings, attached to a waist belt. I keep sunglasses, maps, notebook, pen, granola bar, and cash for the day in this bag. I put my shirt over this bag when I'm in an unsafe area.

I keep the originals of documents with me at all times, even when I shower and sleep. In the shower, I hang my waist pouch on the showerhead. Before I sleep, I put the entire bag under my pillow. Increase your sensitivity by having your security pouch touch your body at all times. Carry all bags, wallets, or purses in front of your body. If you have to carry a wallet, wrap rubber bands around it and slip it deep into a pocket. The rubber will create friction on the fabric of your pocket and make it harder for someone to grab. You will also be more likely to feel the pull. Never, in any event, carry your wallet in your back pocket.

Shoulder bags and backpacks have invisible signs that say *steal me*. On one of my first overseas trips, I ventured into a market town outside Machu Picchu, Peru; I noticed late in the evening that my expensive leather shoulder bag had a slice in the side pocket. I never knew when the thief tried to steal the passport and money I carried in that pocket. A quick cut of the strap, and my bag would have slid into his hands, and off he would go.

Straps should wrap around on your opposite shoulder of where you carry it, not just over your shoulder.

Press on your shoulder bags under your arms when in questionable situations. Distractions or commotions offer thieves the chance to steal from you. In Chichicastenango, Guatemala, I took pictures with both hands on my camera, while my waist pouch remained unguarded and in clear view. A woman came up, pretending to run into me. Within seconds, two people pushed and shoved me. I sensed the belt on my waist pouch tighten, as one of the women tried to pull it off.

I screamed, "Baja, baja, dejeme (stop, stop, leave me alone or go away)!"

My camera airborne, I pushed the women hard while reaching for the camera strap caught between the women and me. Not one person in the market even glanced in my direction during the whole attack

Beware of distractions like someone dropping something in front of you. Step back right away and circle around to see if another person approaches you. Use your instincts. Yell or run if you feel unsafe.

After a few days of carrying all your "stuff" with you everywhere, you might feel how inconvenient it is. In tropical, remote countries, you sweat due to heat and humidity.

Do not let your guard down and decide to stash everything in your daypack while you finish trekking. In the middle of nowhere, safe with a guide, the wind blowing through your clothing, you may feel carefree, with your security belt hidden in your daypack. I know. I experienced this many times.

Your new habits must include discomfort from wearing the belt. Train yourself to feel "naked" without it and find it on your waist when you deplane in your hometown. I travel unknown and isolated paths. My obsession with safety and health sometimes overtakes my adventure. When the heat gets the best of me, or the weight of my packs make me think of drudgery, I remind myself why I came, and I try to find that misplaced carefree attitude.

### *LAPTOPS AND MISCELLANEOUS ELECTRONICS*

If your trip necessitates taking your laptop, iPad, iPod, Kindle, or iPhone, carry the item with you without the case, in a backpack or duffel to keep a low profile. The more you display expensive items, the more you stand out in a crowd. Waiting for planes presents an opportune time to get some work done, but now others know about your electronics.

Do not leave your bags for one second to go check the departure board or to walk to the window to see the young man in the sarong riding the bicycle rickshaw.

Thieves wait for you to leave anything unattended even for a few minutes. Do not ask a stranger to watch your belongings for you.

Do not leave your electronics plugged in during the day while away to recharge them.

Use sites like Carbonite that back up your work, word by word, on computers.

Make CDs or transfer files and photographs of everything on your memory sticks and hide those disks in separate locations, ensuring protection of irreplaceable photographs.

After a trip to a once-in-a-lifetime festival in Papua New Guinea, I opened my little pouch where I kept all my memory sticks for my camera. All four memory sticks were gone. During some fabulous photography opportunity, they fell out.

My stomach felt sick, and I had to stop in my tracks to figure out how to recover from this horrible disaster.

I could not return next year to the same festival. A boring bus ride gave me time to remember copying all the memory sticks onto CDs at an internet café the day before. That precaution saved the day except for the expensive memory sticks I lost.

### *PHONE CARDS*

Phone cards cost more to use abroad, but in many situations, you will have a difficult time finding a telephone center. In central London, a small neighborhood hotel close to the underground offered phone card service, and, after connecting me, the hotel owner said they had to give the pin number to the operator.

Of course, who would ever suspect the charming little woman who had just served you fresh coffee and croissants? When I received my phone bill, I had two hundred dollars' worth of unexplained phone calls the week I spent in Ethiopia, a place where I saw no phones!

When dialing your phone card number, use caution when in public places. I have heard that thieves use binoculars or telephoto lenses to spy on telephone users.

### *FOREIGN LAWS*

Obey foreign laws and remember your guest status in a foreign country. The penalties may surprise you.

Carry identification with you. Your tourist status does not give you the right to break the rules.

If you have had one drink, and you drive in Scandinavian countries, expect uncompromising penalties if you are caught by police.

### *HOMELESS CHILDREN*

In many countries, bands of children surround you outside of transportation depots and hotels. They appear harmless, asking for money and candy. Sometimes they will rob you of jewelry and money without your even realizing it. They employ different tricks, but often they create a commotion around you. Several will get your attention, grabbing either your arms or your luggage, while others search your pockets or bags for valuables. You will not even realize until you return to your room at night that you have missed something or that you have a hole cut in your pocket or bag. Carry everything in front of you. I have yelled when threatened by a group of seemingly harmless children, and they've run away, not wanting to attract the attention of police or adults.

Walking through a market in a border town of Somalia, several children poked and grabbed at me, wanting money. The adults in the area just watched as the children acted more aggressive and started throwing rocks at me. In all my travels, I had never experienced a negative incident or a threat of harm. I refused to leave the area because the families had started to pack their camels for the three-day journey home, and I wanted to watch.

I found protection against a tin shack, but the rocks kept coming my way for a couple of hours. A missionary shopping in the market came my way, directed by a helpful adult who said he had seen a friend with white skin in trouble. He explained the homeless, hungry children had no adults to control them. He rescued me again later that night. In my room, with walls made of mud, I sat on the floor in total darkness, until I was caught off guard by a knock on my door. My flashlight had just died, and I had no matches for my candle. My tent and dinner (a can of tuna) remained packed. A crack in the door exposed the half-lit face of the same missionary who had earlier rescued me at the market. I accepted his offer for dinner with his friends at the mission, and I never forgot his kindness. The five-course meal was the best food I had tasted for more than twenty days, and the conversation topped that. I often think of that missionary and get an itch to write. I want to explain how grateful I felt for his rescue at the market that day and how perfect the timing was for a great meal and a chat with such interesting people.

### *PERSONAL SPACE*

We take for granted our private time driving to work, working at a desk, riding a bicycle, or reading late at night. From our birth, we value personal space. In America, children have their own bedrooms, and adults can walk their dogs or shop for groceries without the annoyances of beggars, homeless children, guides, or curiosity seekers annoying them. When traveling to some countries, finding personal space for alone-time, or just walking through a market without unwanted touches, challenges your patience. Many locals stare at travelers from faraway places, rude in some cultures but not in others. People in other countries may stand closer to each other when talking than we do here in America. Locals also cause discomfort for travelers when in countries where the traveler must watch their every move.

For the most part, people the world over will act as honest and respectful hosts toward you, or I would not continue to travel year after year. Creating personal space influences a part of each of my travel days.

I enjoy walking at sunrise to watch how the locals greet the new day. If the day includes hassles (a lot of stress from a busy market filled with potential thieves, or if I will be climbing a dangerous cliff), I make sure to spend some time in relaxing quiet time, cuddled in my sleeping bag with my journal and headphones, listening to my favorite music from home. In Mopti, Mali, the security guards standing at the gates of my hotel helped me to escape the bothersome young men annoying tourists for money. I ran into a friend I had met on the flight from New York and asked him to share some of his adventures so far. He said he was fed up with the constant demands from these boys, wanting him to pay for all kinds of services--like helping him cross the street for a twenty-dollar fee. He sat on my hotel patio and said he missed finding personal space more than anything else in Mali.

### *GIVING IN TO CRIME*

When confronted by an assailant, no matter your location, give him whatever he asks. If you give the thief some money and your cheap drugstore watch, he will leave with more than he could make in a month of working. Lose a little money rather than take the chance of injury by arguing with the assailant.

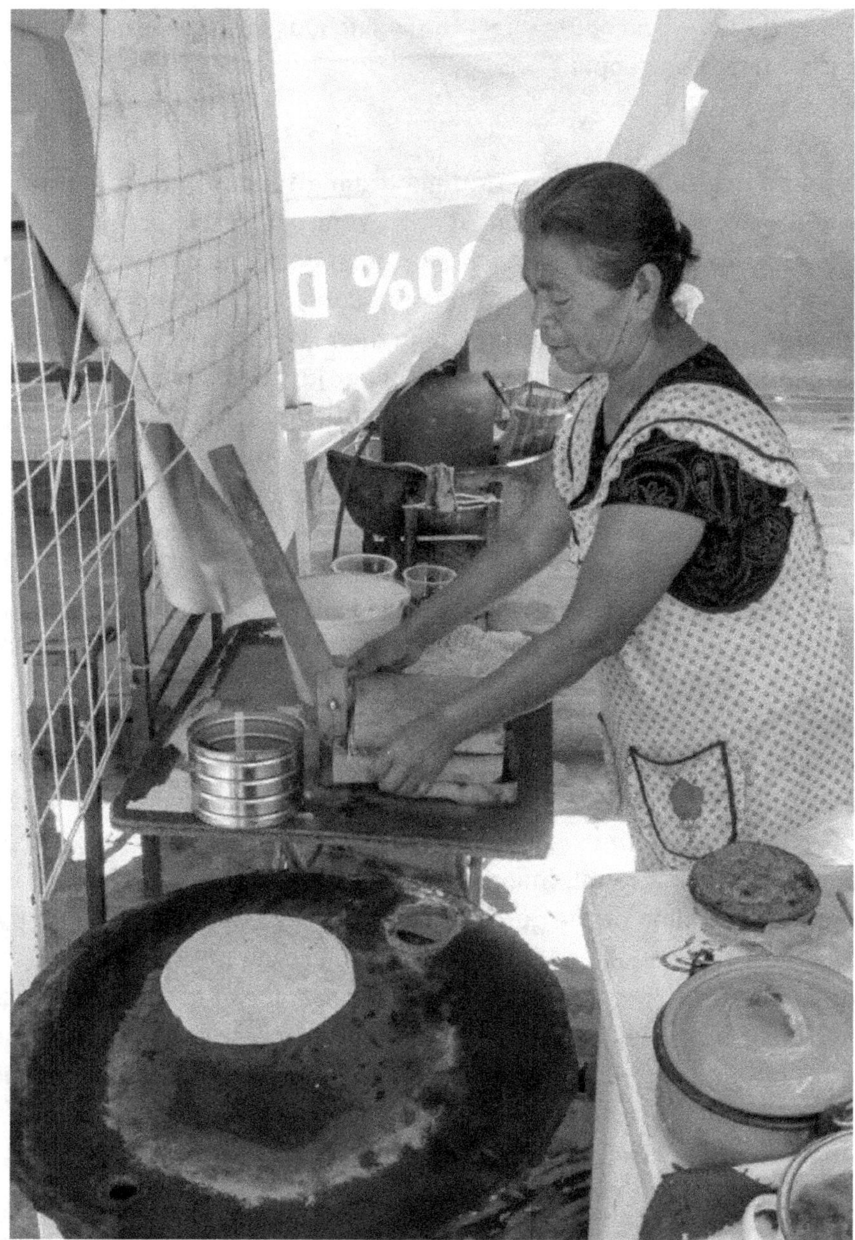

*13. Atotonilco woman making tortillas, Mexico*

Robbers can get violent if you give them nothing. I have traveled alone for over forty years. I have only felt my life threatened one time in all those years. Driving into the virgin jungle to find the lip-disk-wearing Mursi tribe, we came upon three naked men who stopped our vehicle. They pointed AK-7s at us, and demanded a few coins to let us pass. Maybe the guns were not loaded, and maybe they would have backed off if we refused to pay. My driver didn't take that risk.

***TAKE A POSITIVE ATTITUDE***

Many books and articles discuss safety on the internet, a good place to look if you want to find out more about how to handle terrorism, assault, heart attacks, exposure to contagious diseases, oil spills, lost tickets, etc.

Horror stories lurk around every corner. They educate you but should not prevent you from traveling. Some dangers lie outside your control, and you may never face the bizarre ones.

To avoid the common ones and those you have the ability to prevent, you need to prepare ahead for them. After choosing your destination and researching the potential hazards of that country, you must take into account that risks exist for natives and tourists alike. If you adopt a positive attitude, you can make your trip work.

Most crimes abroad occur during one's off-guard moments. Leaving something unguarded for a second can trigger an opportunist's temptation. Think about this: a pair of sunglasses might take him a month to earn; why wouldn't he make a play for them?

Instead of making yourself vulnerable to theft, leave the designer glasses and expensive watch at home.

Try not to let the strangeness of your new environment upset you. Whether you have the ability to do something or not do something, do not second-guess or fret about your decision. A friend, Paul Marnett, once said to me, "All of our frustrations come, not from the frustration itself, but from not having the ability to comprehend the reason for the frustration."

If you find yourself in trouble, stop, take a deep breath, and take control. My situation with the homeless children helps explain what I mean. Instead of running to my room and hiding the rest of the day, I stayed, waiting for something positive to come of the day. The way you think influences the reality of your experiences. In other words, your positive attitude will bring on positive manifestations. Listen to your inner self. You have internal warning systems. Look confident but anticipate anything. Within yourself, you can find the power to travel in safety.

# Chapter 10: ethics and communications

*"The world is like a mask dancing. If you want to see it well, you do not stand in one place."* Ghanaian proverb

***RESPONSIBLE TRAVEL***

To leave home for the far corners of the world means intruding into someone else's reality. Travelers will notice the differences in the day-to-day activities of locals compared to daily routines in their home countries. A foreign countryman's pride and thought go into everyday tasks that we take for granted.

We respond to the greeting of, "How are you," with, "I am fine." In countries with a slower pace than our own, a handshake and a greeting can last several minutes. You have a better-quality trip when you treat other cultures and their customs with sensitivity. Use your senses to detect the subtle changes in customs. The level of your reception by foreigners improves with your positive attitude, friendliness, and respect for them and their culture.

You touch their existence with your modern-day technology. As a guest in another culture, you do not have the right to judge their ethics. As a traveler, you have to know the impact you will have on the culture you visit. In less industrialized countries, a community's subsistence comes from the land and each other. Exposure to materialist things that these people do not have creates a desire within them to have those things.

Primitive societies adapt to the sun's harsh rays with handmade rice paste for sunscreen. And rustic musical instruments encourage group singing and hold a community together. However, a tribal teenager seeing sunglasses and a MP3 player may develop doubt about his own circumstances, beginning with confusion and humiliation. Our relative wealth, important jobs, and higher education give us the ability to explore unfamiliar territory; they do not give us permission to abuse our privileges as a guest of another country.

Recognizing and appreciating the differences between cultures define the sensitive traveler. The casual tourist, with no regard for dress codes, respect for religious customs or appropriate behavior, will never touch the heart of a resident of a foreign country. Do not miss opportunities to gain a richer understanding of other cultures. Respecting other peoples' worldviews can peel away layers of resentment built by previous cultural trespassers. The smallest of helpful deeds can leave behind friendships for a lifetime.

Respecting the traditions and customs of a country will help to ensure a higher level of safety. In some countries, you offend people and even break the law when you dress or behave in a crude or inappropriate manner. For example, in Singapore, you can expect fines when you break the law by dropping a cigarette butt on the sidewalk.

A violation of dress codes has consequences in some regions like the Middle East. A woman wearing a short skirt or shorts, a revealing bikini, or a tank top attracts negative attention, and she could be arrested. Blend in with the community by wearing comfortable clothing that fits in with your current surroundings. Do not wear anything that causes you to stand out such as loud or unusual jewelry, hats, or clothing. Find out about dress codes before you arrive in a city. By keeping a low profile and blending in, you will encounter fewer risks.

I received an invitation to a ceremony at a palace on the Island of Bali. The invitation called for traditional dress. Not having a clue as to what to wear, I typed in the name of the ceremony online to see photographs of others attending the same type of ceremony. I decided that I needed to wear a kebayah (traditional Balinese blouse) and sarong (long length of fabric wound tight like a skirt). The kebayah was made of lace, either pure white or tinted with contrasting colors. I e-mailed an author who lived in Bali, who mentioned that ceremony in one of her books. She gave me an idea of where to shop upon arrival. Several women from local shops gave me ideas on what to wear, and my appearance at the ceremony fit right in with the outfits worn by the other guests.

Food customs vary regarding what you eat, and how you eat it. Guidebooks will suggest restaurants that serve American food if you do not seek adventure. Trying new foods and eating with your fingers has rewards, along with allowing you to meet new friends at the same time. Do not offend the locals by challenging customs and demanding utensils if they are not offered.

When you have a problem with the language barrier, keep in mind your responsibility as a guest. You have to figure out how to communicate. Instead of wondering if the joke they are telling is about you, try to figure out the context of their words. Darkness falls, you feel lost, and a stranger ignores your pleas for help with your map. He waves you away. Embarrassed by and disgusted with these foreigners and this town, you lose your patience. But wait: instead of becoming angry, you need to remind yourself that you intruded upon the lives of these people, and you do not want to frighten them with your language. Respect the privacy of locals with whom you come into contact. If you seek help from one person and he will not give it, smile and find someone else more willing to help.

As the foreigner, you interrupted the routine of somebody's life. Make sure that your behavior is such that the next person does not mind when you show him your map.

My daughter Allie and I listened to Ismael, our guide, explain the millions of microscopic organisms known as *dinoflagellates* that sparkle when disturbed in La Parguera Phosphorescent Bay. The bay surrounded us in a peaceful darkness, except for Ismael kicking his feet in the water, causing millions of diamond-like lights to sparkle. Off the coast of Puerto Rico, able to enjoy this rare and unusual phenomenon, the three of us jumped in the water. Four tourists at the back of our boat talked about which preschool to enroll their toddlers in. The others argued over the advantages of their best choices for education, as we noticed white sparkles covering our arms. I will never forget the magic of that night. The first time seeing this extraordinary mystery with my entire family while sailing around Vieques, I refused to get in the water. Those four young parents did exactly what I'd done: they'd failed to appreciate the uniqueness of this island.

### ***BODY LANGUAGE***

Nonverbal communication varies from country to country just like verbal skills. Gestures, posture, eye contact, and facial expressions all speak a silent language.

Keep your distance from people in other cultures; avoid touching, and forget hugging unless familiar with the customs. Show a smile for a greeting instead of shaking hands. In Thailand, touching someone's head could lead to a misunderstanding.

The head, the highest part of the body, is given respect, as it is the home of the spirit and soul. The touching of someone's head except by grandparents to small children results in inappropriate glances and considered taboo.

Siblings do not touch their parents' heads. People avoid passing things over other people's heads, and if one touches someone's head by mistake, an apology is necessary. In countries like India, the Middle East, and in parts of Africa, shaking hands or eating with your left hand will mark you as disrespectful. The Japanese avoid all physical contact, while in Latin American countries, you see people hugging all the time. Superficial customs might confuse you, but you need to understand them to keep from insulting your hosts.

Using common everyday nonverbal signs requires caution. The "gimme-five" gesture in some countries will come across as very negative as well as our thumbs up sign of "everything's okay." Even a friendly nod of your head can mean the opposite of yes.

Maintain a positive mental attitude and control your behavior. Observe the local customs and try not to stand out in a crowd with an inappropriate attitude, making fun of local customs or dress. Use respect toward the laws and customs, which will help to bridge the cultural gap between your world and theirs.

### *TIPPING*

Tipping in a foreign country can be a puzzling situation. Comments about local customs appear in guidebooks, but in most cases, you will have to rely on your own instincts.

Restaurants will often include tips in the price of the meal except in more remote reaches of the world where tipping does not exist. In general, 10 to 20 percent would work for waiters, bartenders, room service, and hairstylists.

For all the other assorted help, you receive from parking lot attendants, housekeepers, concierge, door attendants, to shuttle drivers, and tour guides, you will have to use your best judgment. If you do not tip, show your appreciation with a thank you.

If you are in doubt as to how much or when to tip, ask the local people for advice or check with the employees of your hotel. Parts of Africa, Asia, China, and the Malaysian countries do not practice tipping.

Some countries consider it an insult to tip, and in other countries it may be illegal.

Try not to over-tip, as this makes things hard on the next tourist. A ten percent tax and five percent service charge will appear in most every restaurant bill on the island of Bali.

No tips expected. Porters and cab drivers expect tips according to the number of pieces of luggage they carry. As in the United States, guides, door attendants, and drivers expect tips in many countries.

### *BEGGING*

Those of us who live in larger cities see homeless people and beggars standing on street corners with signs asking for "food for work." We see surprising scenes of begging in other parts of the world, too. When we travel, beggars tempt us, and we do not know what to do, as we stretch our funds to get more out of our trip. In the less industrialized countries, government programs to assist older or crippled citizens do not exist.

Perhaps begging presents a survival solution for those outcasts (the crippled, weak, and elderly). I have heard, in some countries, mothers cripple their children and send them to the streets to beg for food or money. This attitude teaches children to grow up never realizing the importance of contributing to society. Let your instincts dictate when and how much. One of the few times I gave in to begging, I learned a lesson. A homeless woman and two children drew my sympathy, and I handed her a couple of dollars on a Mexican side street. I exited the shop across the street a few minutes later to find the three of them eating candy bars and drinking sodas. My hopes for that money? Maybe three nutritious meals of protein and vegetables.

### *COMMUNICATIONS*

Living in the twenty-first century, we take for granted our incredible communication systems. Cell phones, fax machines, computers, e-mail, and the Internet have changed how we function. Our telephones take our messages, tell us who called, and put on hold another call when we are too busy checking stock quotes. Keeping in touch, like safety, will rank high with travelers when they leave home.

Maintaining contact could mean a phone call or e-mail message, depending on the country you visit. In less developed countries, you will have to figure out how to contact those at home, or resign yourself to traveling without communication for long periods. In today's world, internet cafés appear everywhere. In a small, rural village in southern China, I found a little house with several computers used for games for the teenagers of the village. They had access to the Internet but did not know what to do with it except find games. While I caught up with friends and relatives, the sounds of racecars and swords swooshing back and forth came from every direction. Skype is also available in some surprising places around the world.

### *TELEPHONES*

We get used to telephones as teenagers, talking and texting for hours into the night. As adults, we plant phones in convenient spaces like bedrooms, kitchens, and bathrooms. The cell phones in our pockets or handbags allow us to manage several tasks at the same time. Teenagers object when teachers award detentions for phones ringing during class time, and adults complain when calls drop while they are conducting business on cells. This all changes when we travel away from modern society. We need flexibility when trying to adapt to the antiquated equipment we might use while traveling. Phones can present challenges. The symbols on dials and buttons are hard to understand, and require a foreign coin or token. In addition, operators speak the local language blurred by loud static.

Each country has a unique phone system. Use it when you travel in the larger cities. In Third and Fourth World countries, do not depend on finding a phone once you leave the capital city. Many smaller Third World cities have phone centers that open certain times of the day. These centers are often busy, and cash is expected as payment. NEVER count on posted phone center hours.

### *CELL PHONES*

Staying in touch with family and friends by using a cell phone while traveling can present practical challenges. If demands from a job require you to call on a regular basis, you will have to compromise your trip. The provider can tell you if cell phone service works for your travel plans or if you must consider this a time to enjoy the peace and quiet.

I can't get used to seeing people selling cell phone time on the streets. While in Cartagena, Columbia, I saw a cell phone octopus. A man stood with cords coming from every direction out of one small piece of equipment, and at the end of each cord, he had attached a cell phone. For a few coins each, several people talked or texted at the same time on different phones.

Cell phone technology evolves at the speed of light. In many countries if you have a phone that uses a sim card, you can buy a local sim card and insert it into your phone for local use and pay upfront for minutes. Plan, and apprise loved ones and friends of your itinerary and how long it will take until you can call again. Cheap SIM cards can enhance your own or rental phones, and booths in markets offer excellent deals. Check with your carrier to find the rules of how to activate that service. Outside a CircleK convenience store in Bali, a girl had cheap rental cell phones and SIM cards for sale.

### *LAPTOPS, NOTEBOOKS AND iPADS*

Portable computers can present problems on a trip. Sending and receiving information may keep your business on the right track while away. Hand-carry your laptop wherever you go. Protecting your computer from the problems of theft and the elements of the environment will require your attention 24/7. Extra batteries tend to be heavy, and finding the right converters for electrical outlets with the right voltage can present a challenge. Check the Internet to find the appropriate adapter and converter, if needed. Take an extension cord with you and an adapter that allows three grounded plugs for use at one time. Also, take a plug that adapts from a grounded plug to a non-grounded plug. In undeveloped countries, electrical outlets sit next to a light switch, or other strange locations, at shoulder height. By the time you plug in an adapter plug or converter box, a grounded to non-grounded single plug, a grounded three plug-in adapter and then have three appliances hanging off that (like chargers for camera batteries, computer, and an extension cord), the weight will pull everything to the floor. Bring some masking tape or duct tape along with you when you travel so you can tape the heavy plugs to the wall and keep them plugged in.

You can expect to use electronic mail worldwide and Wi-Fi signs hang on guesthouse entrances all over the world. Larger Internet cafes offer printing, fax, and copy services (including making CDs and DVDs from your camera's full memory sticks). After traipsing through deserts or jungles, do not expect to find Internet in your grass hut though! Keep in mind that in Third and Fourth world countries, people cannot afford to waste resources. Be sensitive to this when communicating with family and friends back home while using the computers of natives in the country you are visiting. Let me give you an example of what I mean. After twenty-some days in remote Ethiopia, I came to the capital city and stayed with a friend of a friend. She had received some messages from my office and family, and I asked her to print them for me, never considering the cost of paper. The lady could not believe I wanted to use up her precious resources. I waste more paper at home, printing a week's worth of articles to read later than they use in a year's time. Embarrassed, I told her not to bother making me copies for later and read my messages then and there.

### *GLOBAL POSITIONING SYSTEMS*

GPS navigation involves the science of maps, itineraries, and geographic accuracy. Your remote travels will take you away from mapped trails and villages, but hiring a guide who knows the area well will help give you peace of mind in finding the way back. Research can aid you in finding how long and far away from help your sojourn will take you. For persons unfamiliar with the terrain, landmarks will begin to disappear. After many weeks of travel after leaving civilization and being exposed to weather, changes in diet, and physical fatigue, your confusion increases. A GPS unit (either a stand-alone unit or one within your cell phone), can keep you on track.

The GPS displays altitude, longitude, latitude, time of sunrise and much more, information that it receives from orbiting satellites. Consider the cost of getting lost in a desert or dangerous area compared to the modest investment in a GPS unit. You will need to recharge the device regularly, so remember that when you are off the beaten path overseas, finding electrical outlets and working automobile cigarette lighters might be a problem. Foreign countries do not always have available power sources, even in more populated areas, and if you are an adventure traveler and often in remote areas, your recharging options will be even harder to find. Make sure you research GPS recharging options before leaving home.

After extensive research, I located a map identifying many of the tribes of southern Ethiopia. The driver I hired used my map and tried to follow the dry riverbeds serving as roads. This proved a real test for his Toyota Land Cruiser. Having never traveled this area, I needed to create landmarks along the way so we could get back. In my GPS unit, I recorded landmarks throughout my trip. I entered locations of bridges, mud huts, and giant baobab trees with the appropriate mileage along the way. I kept track of the altitude at these landmarks and the time of day. The GPS can store all this information, so you can turn around and find your way back if lost. Years later, you can find that hidden tribe which took days to discover, simply by using your GPS! Look up the directions and print out your trip.

### *FAXES*

A fax can help you send paperwork to another country. This way, time zone changes do not affect your messages. Some countries do not understand the concept of faxes and charge you ridiculous rates, so ask first. At the grand Ethiopian Hotel in downtown Addis Ababa, the hotel clerk wanted twelve dollars for a one-line message to my bank. Bad phone lines and line noise interfere with faxes. Keeping a message short offers a better opportunity to get the message through between interruptions or line noise. You can send faxes between the power outages, but you have little chance of receiving faxes with electricity going on and off daily. An international hotel may have a direct international satellite fax number.

### *MAIL SERVICES*

Postcards serve as a cheap way to say hello to friends. Do not expect them to arrive home before you do unless your trip lasts more than three weeks, or you mail them from a large, developed city. Use stamps from the country where purchased. Finding post offices in larger cities of less-developed countries sometimes wastes a half-day or more. When you do get there, either they close before the closing hours posted, or nobody works behind the counter. Often hotels will sell stamps for postcards and mail them for you. Most countries have reliable mail service. For addresses, use block capital letters in countries where the local language has a different alphabet. Insist that they cancel all stamps in your presence in less-developed countries because, if not, after you leave, they might remove the stamps and resell them. Postal workers may earn less than the value of the stamps themselves.

### *MEASUREMENT UNITS*

The metric system of units prevails in every country except the United States and its territories. When traveling abroad, think in metric units instead of trying to convert to US equivalents. If you can think in metric terms, you then know the real value of items. The Celsius temperature scale challenges your memory, so keep track of basic comparisons. I seek warmth when I hear zero degrees Celsius, which converts to thirty-two degrees Fahrenheit. When I hear thirty degrees Celsius, which is eighty-six degrees Fahrenheit, I am in heaven.

### *TIME*

Tickets, clocks, and signs use twenty-four-hour time everywhere in the world, except in the United States. The ambiguous practice of twelve-hour time confuses foreigners visiting the United States, causing them to miss flights and appointments.

A restaurant may post hours of operation as 7:00 to 1:00. A foreigner would not know if that meant breakfast from 0700 to 1300 or dinner from 1900 to 0100.

### *CALENDARS*

For business and schedules, most countries use the Christian calendar even if they use a different calendar for religious purposes. The dominant religion of a country determines when offices and shops close. In Christian countries, many businesses close on Sundays. Israel's national airline, El Al, at one time grounded flights on their Sabbath, which is Saturday. In the United States, some states do not sell alcohol on Sundays.

Business hours stated in guidebooks are not always accurate. Business hours change due to changes in business ownership, etc. Some businesses will close after lunch for naptime, like in many South American countries. Some businesses close during dinner hour.

In the United States, we write our dates in the order of the month, day, and year.

The rest of the world puts the day before the month and year. Therefore, dates can be confusing for Americans making hotel, flight, or tour reservations for travel abroad. Some English-speaking travel agents and airline employees adopt the order of day, month, and year.

### *CALCULATORS*

Shop owners and bank employees that cater to foreigners use electronic calculators to conduct business and show conversions.

Showing your ignorance by not reading a price tag, or by not understanding a quoted price in a foreign language, labels you as a vulnerable tourist.

Understanding the exchange rate will give you better negotiating power. Often the seller will hand the calculator to the buyer with the suggested price. Either party will negotiate and ask, “What’s your best price?”

### *FOREIGN LANGUAGES*

Learning even a few basic words in the language of the country of your travels will pay off. Those words will help you get around with less effort, and your choices expand when you can communicate with even a minimum of words. The person you meet may not know English, and even in countries where English prevails as the second language, you will find yourself in situations where nobody can communicate with you. Guidebooks and phrasebooks can offer the basics to help you get along for short trips of two or three weeks. The Internet will help you find translations for hundreds of languages.

Sometimes, in Spanish speaking countries, I try to order food or bargain with a few Spanish words, usually mispronounced. Better to try to communicate in the local language than not to try at all. People look down on Americans who assume that everyone around the world should speak English. I think people have pride in their individual cultures and appreciate your willingness to try to communicate in their native tongue. Communicating with a limited understanding of a language can make you feel intimidated. If you make mistakes, be confident, willing to look a little foolish, and try again.

Be considerate when foreigners try to help you, and be patient and understanding when they give you a room for one instead of two, or when they deliver the wrong food item to your table. If you do not speak their language, reverse roles, and imagine someone asking you for directions in Swahili. Avoid making sarcastic jokes; foreigners do not understand our sarcasm and may be extremely offended by it. Use eye contact when negotiating. Find simple words for communication. Some people lack the confidence to speak English with you but can understand what you say. If possible, show an interest in your host's culture or area, make positive comments about the environment, or pronounce with confidence the President's or Prime Minister's name. This will go a long way toward building a relationship with people of other countries. Even the barest minimum of speaking a foreign language will change the whole flavor of your trip and can open doors otherwise closed. In your conversations, politeness and kindness will help show respect for the people and their culture.

### *FINDING HELP*

Many agencies can help you in an emergency when abroad. A Consulate helps with matters that concern their own citizens in foreign countries, while

Embassies deal with diplomatic matters. If you find yourself in a difficult situation, contact the nearest U.S. Consulate Office. When traveling in a country with civil unrest or any other danger, you might want to register with the U.S. Consulate or U.S. Embassy. This allows family members back home to find you in case of an emergency back home. In case of evacuation, the embassy can contact you. These offices have no attorneys and cannot get you out of jail. They can find you legal representation, however.

An American consular office can advise you of your rights, help you to get in touch with relatives or friends, and assure you receive money wired to you. They also offer a vital source of information through help services.

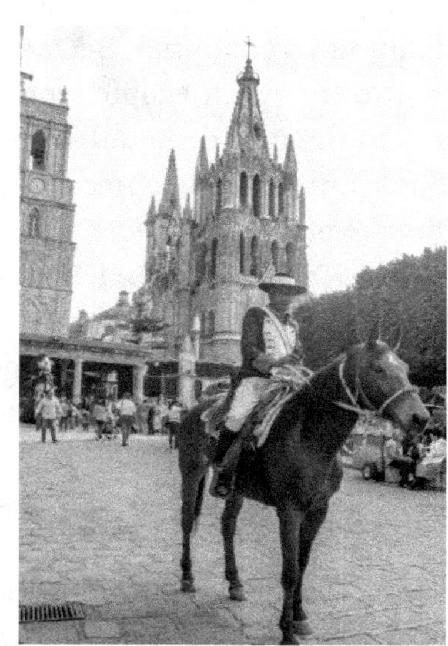

*14. Local policeman, San Miguel de Allende, Mexico*

### *DO NOT FORGET*

Copy your key addresses, passwords to online accounts, and phone numbers in your journal. How soon you will forget your best friend's phone number when you wait in line for three hours in a Singapore telephone center, and then you get the authorization to make that call. Leave a detailed itinerary with relatives or friends before you leave home. As your plans change, keep those at home informed of your location. Buy many postcards as reminders of your experiences. Keep a journal or at least take notes. Journals help to pass the time when you are waiting for food, planes, etc. They help you maintain awareness of even the smallest of details. Reading your notes months later will bring back the details of your trip. Photos, plus those notes, will bring experiences to life in full color, which memory alone cannot do. Do not forget to print a blank calendar for the month and enter names of hotels and their locations as you travel.

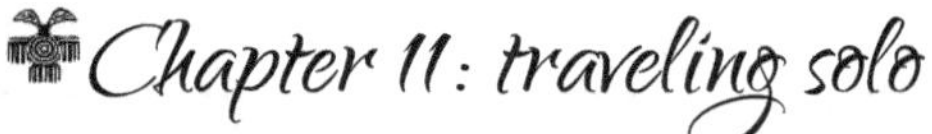

# Chapter 11: traveling solo

*"It is difficult today to leave one's friends and family ... and yet, when it is done, I find there is a vitality to being alone that is incredibly precious. Life rushes back into the void, richer, more vivid, and fuller than before."*
Anne Morrow Lindbergh

***PROS AND CONS***

Traveling alone, you let your courage open the doors to a different experience. Find the birth of a newfound confidence. Personal beliefs predict behaviors. This binds you with confidence when considering your options. Believing in your intuition promotes resourcefulness for tackling problems and conflicts as they happen. Responsibility to no one but yourself steadies you with feelings of personal security. Companions act as fragments of your homeland, glued to you with gossip, mood swings, and decision-making powers of their own.

Traveling alone sparks curiosity about the local people. Instead of sharing a bond with a partner while discussing the attitudes of the people or second-guessing the whys of their culture, you find yourself seeking the answers to those questions with the people themselves. My journals are filled with stories of encounters with local people that ended in laughter, hugs, and warm feelings. While exploring the strange boat-shaped homes of a Tana Toraja village, I noticed an old man staring at me from his second story window. He waved me inside. I climbed the vertical steps to find him sitting Indian-style on a vinyl mat next to a pack of cigarettes, a thermos, and a cup. He tried on my sunglasses, looked through my viewfinder, and took a photo of me, much to his delight. He had not smiled until the moment he took the photo. He never spoke a word, but somehow translated a story about a designated sleeping area for young couples wanting to conceive a baby. He used his hands, pointed to himself and me, and made motions of lovemaking and then motions of swaddling or rocking a baby and a sad face for crying and tears. I had an apple and some nuts to share, to show my appreciation, but he bowed as he left with his hands together to say, "Namaste," or "Thank you for becoming my friend" My guide later told me I guessed correctly about the special area used to conceive a baby, and he envied my luck in meeting a man with such contentment.

Traveling alone allows us the opportunity to see with our own eyes. When traveling with others, in order to please them, we settle for what they want us to see. Partners compromise our reactions to the world, as we adjust our perceptions to allow for acceptance from those partners. The partner takes on the job of determining how we should act.

Alone, we sense an obligation to interact with those around us speaking the local language. A partner sharing our language slows us down because we have someone to share communication. A partner provides a bubble, like a sterile safety net.

A list of key incentives for traveling alone would have to include the freedom of choice. Spontaneous opportunities arise on any trip like meeting someone wanting to show you how to build a kite. So spend a few days kite-building, and then head to the beach to fly it. For years, I had to rationalize why I would leave my home behind for travel to remote societies to think, to take part, or to watch. After all, I am just a woman! Once I accepted myself, it seemed to make the resistance others felt toward my travel unimportant. The quiet solitude of traveling alone reveals to you perceptions about your own character. More awareness of the little details helps you make a connection with this vast world. This compelling awareness increases ten-fold when you're alone. Traveling alone is like jumping off a bridge and building your wings on the way down. You learn to soar above previous fears, accepting humility and kindness learned from newfound friends.

Thomas Jefferson once said, "One travels more usefully when alone because he reflects more."

Recent statistics say one in four Americans, who travel, do so alone. Singles account for $2.2 trillion in annual buying power. Twenty-five million singles over forty-two spent over twenty-eight billion in travel in 2008.

We travel alone by choice, a bit like a journey into our inner selves. We could have a love or hate relationship with ourselves, determined by the challenges of traveling alone, otherwise we find ourselves wanting to return to the familiarity home or for companionship, we cling to strangers we meet on our journey. If we have made the decision to travel alone, we probably know ourselves pretty well.

Being a loner has nothing to do with loneliness. Times arise while you're traveling when you want to share that purple sunset or the sounds of tribal men, chanting in the distance. When we set out to travel alone, we think we can leave the emotional difficulties of life behind. Forking out dollars and time, we start with the attitude that a trip will remind us of Christmas, with presents to open along the way. However, we may have incredible lonely spells. With our source of strength left behind, we feel unknown, lonesome, uncared for, in strange and peculiar surroundings. We bring our sustenance for our journey, never dreaming that part of our existence depends on the emotional support we receive from loved ones. The quality of our experiences depends on the emotional balance we place on ourselves during the trip. Watch over yourself, and figure out ways to lift your spirits if depression catches you by surprise.

Henry David Thoreau once said that, "The man who travels alone can start today; but he who travels with another must wait 'till that other is ready."

The advantages of traveling alone FAR outweigh the disadvantages. When you travel with someone, you spend your time talking and interacting with that person. You spend time making that partner happy. Yes, they share the experience of watching the children flying kites on the shores of the Rio Napo River, but if you are alone, the children will accept your presence and invite you to join them.

When traveling alone, you will reach out to the local people for their conversation and company. Alone, you seem less threatening and more approachable to people of other cultures. When alone, you interact with strangers more readily. You decide where to go and how long to stay there, not depending on the wishes of a partner. You integrate into the reality of the cultures you visit, since that defines why you traveled there. Leaving your friends and customs behind will bring you closer to accepting new cultures while visiting them.

### *SPECIAL SITUATIONS*

Use the Internet to find dozens of sites dedicated to travel for singles. Search for sites that connect you with other single travelers like Solo Travel Network at www.cstn.org. Many tour companies offer single-only trips (for instance, Windjammer has sailing trips for singles). Norwegian Cruise Lines offers single rooms on their ship *Epic*, with a private lounge for those in the single cabins.

### *DEALING WITH LONELINESS*

A sidewalk café, showcasing locals walking along the street in colorful sarongs and balancing baskets on their heads, offers a peaceful spot for reflecting on the incredible sights you've seen. The fascination of travel can sometimes begin to fade after a few days of wandering farming villages, sitting on the beach watching fishermen unloading their day's work, or peering behind hidden walls of old ruins. Questions arise, such as, "Am I just taking a detour from my life or trying to escape my responsibilities?" Remind yourself of the reasons why you needed this journey in your life.

If you recognize the need to reconnect with family in the States, then find an internet café or phone home. Writing postcards allows you to feel productive and share your experiences.

Start a conversation with a stranger, sitting across from you at a cafe. Although you may find it hard to converse with strangers at home, you will find a natural camaraderie between you and strangers abroad. Foreigners seek other foreigners. Americans sometimes believe that the whole world should speak English, so I do not want anyone to think I am an ugly American with assumptions. I try to start a conversation with, "Where are you from?" Often people reply, "I do not speak English." Challenge yourself and muster up the confidence to respond because nobody will judge you.

Take things with you that remind you of home, loved ones, and the reality you left behind. Photographs take little space.

I download my favorite songs onto my iPod or thumb drive. Listening to music before I sleep comforts me like a security blanket from home.

Go shopping, even if your list of "to-dos" does not include spending money. Explore extraordinary local markets. Surrounded by crowds of people, you will not even think of loneliness. Just sitting on a curb, you begin people watching, creating a fascinating scene. The bustling activity never ceases, and you can learn so much about a culture while wandering in and out of the little alleyways of a market.

Hang out at the local restaurant for travelers like yourself. Do not let your lack of knowledge cause paranoia. If the language barrier bothers you, or you do not know where the next path should lead, go for a walk, and then sleep on it. The answers will come to you.

Ask around for ideas on something different to do. Rent a moped or bicycle, and discover the nooks and crannies of the town. Ride a horse up to the hot springs you read about the night before. Try to find the shop of a local artisan and ask to watch him or her at work. Your guidebook will list suggestions.

Check bulletin boards in cafes and travelers' hotels for ongoing classes or someone looking for a partner to share a kayak for a few days.

Take a blank notebook and keep a journal. When bored or lonesome, describe the reactions to your senses. Paint a word picture of all the elements that made up your dinner. What do you remember as you sampled the food? Reflections of the day will inspire you to write, write, and write. After your return home, reading your diary will help you recall those moments in colorful detail. When you think about the experiences that went into making up your days abroad, you will have difficulty remembering each one. The smells. The natives dancing. The songs. Some will return to your mind, triggered by a word or a suddenly remembered face. Your journal will help keep all the pieces interlocked, overlapped, and blended like a mosaic.

### *WOMEN ALONE*

If a woman does her research on cultural attitudes, she can go anywhere in the world. Cultural, political, and religious attitudes toward women should not limit destinations. Women traveling alone often deal with cultural sensitivity much more than men. Some cultures view independent women traveling alone as inappropriate behavior. Understanding the correct social behavior will help keep women from hassles with men. Exposed to life different from our accustomed ways, we open ourselves to vulnerability. Unique challenges face a woman traveling alone, much more so than for groups of women or for men traveling alone. Because you do not have a local's understanding of the culture, your dependence on your own instincts may misguide you. Though still believing it an oddity to see a woman traveling alone, humankind has a natural respect for women, which gives women an open door into cultures that men might not access. Do your homework. Try to understand, before you go, the social customs and status of women of the areas in which you travel.

In choosing whom you spend time with, you will need to use discretion. I find the most annoying part of traveling alone as a woman is the annoyance factor that men put on you. Sometimes a sincere smile or just eye contact from me can suggest to a man that I wish to make advances or need his assistance. In some countries, men have stuck to me like leeches, and I could not even burn them off with words or body language. You may find that after trying to disappear into shops, you come back out onto the street and there are men waiting outside the door for you. Their unrelenting pursuit can wear you out as you repeat the word *no* to their suggestions.

In my travels, I have faced this challenge often with young entrepreneurs thinking I needed their services. In Mali, West Africa, a group of boys surrounded me day and night. They sat beside me in restaurants, at the bank, and in cabs or buses. Numerous times, I tried to ditch them in markets and down little alleyways. However, my white skin made it hard to blend in. After a few days of my saying, "No, go away," the boys would all repeat the phrase at the same time as they followed me. Sitting on the banks of the River Niger, I would take out my notepad and start writing. At some point, the boys would eventually all leave, allowing me to absorb life on the river. Once the boys were gone, I could pull out my friend, my camera. Time after time the fishing nets flew into the air, dropped deep to touch the muddy river bottom, and swished out again. Finding a bit of personal space, I could compose myself and reflect on my extraordinary day.

Your way of natural friendliness or even flirting converts to offensive behavior in some cultures. Try to watch the interaction between males and females at the beginning of your trip. Traveling alone, you become a conversation piece, appraised as either peculiar, independent, or easy. "Western women" have a reputation for being wild and independent in many foreign countries, and it is believed that they sometimes travel to meet foreign lovers. Prepare to suffer the consequences if you take the attitude of dressing and acting as you please. American women can act like the most independent women I have ever met. In many parts of the world, especially in those conservative countries of the Middle East, women gain a bad reputation by their dress and behavior. In some cultures, wearing shorts or jeans invites cold stares, gossip regarding your morality, and perhaps increased vulnerability. Exposed legs may invite sexual thoughts to men who might take that as a sign of a prostitute.

Pay attention to what women wear and modify your wardrobe to fit various situations. This means wearing long sleeve shirts and long pants or a skirt, and sometimes a hat or scarf to cover your head in Islamic countries. I carry a sarong, which I can wrap over my pants, around my shoulders, or on my head when I'm uncomfortable with people staring at me. If you dress like the local women, you'll blend in, earn respect, and achieve a low profile. Rather than have suspicions surrounding you, make smart choices and stick with them.

Never stare at a man for any length of time. In most cultures, including our own, that encourages an invitation. Casual encounters or conversations may lead to surprises in a different way than you expect. A man may leave you with the idea of showing up in your hotel room later that night. Watch what you say and think about your reactions to his suggestions.

Show confidence. Know your destination and prove that you can take care of yourself.

If you have to ask for help with directions, stop in a shop or cafe. Holding your map wide open on a street advertises your need. Do not let anyone take advantage of your ignorance. Your lost look invites strangers to approach you. Stay away from deserted streets or swimming pools at night and try to keep people around you. Stay alert to the sound of footsteps behind you. Know how to contact the local police.

If, while you're listening to local street musicians in the town square, you are interrupted by bothersome men wanting to buy you coffee, then, with diplomacy, ask them to leave.

That space belongs to you, and you have every right to ask them to leave without offending anyone.

I do not suggest that you ignore all male strangers during your explorations. Use common sense when choosing with whom to spend time. Consider the effect your behavior and your manner of dress will have on men with whom you come into contact.

These determine the outcome of how they treat you in return. Dealing with unwanted behavior requires common sense and a little advance preparation.

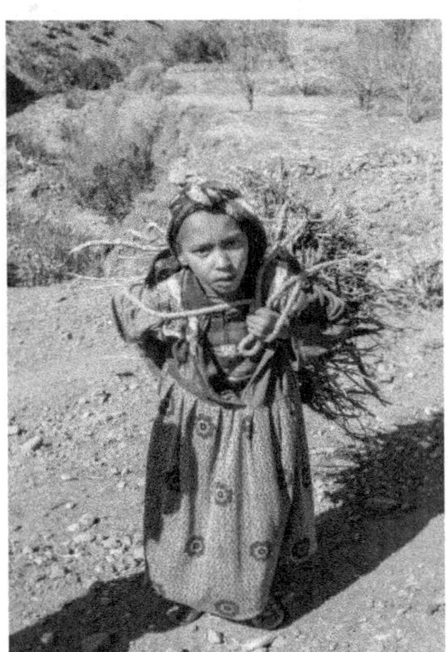

*15. Carrying firewood down from hills, Morocco*

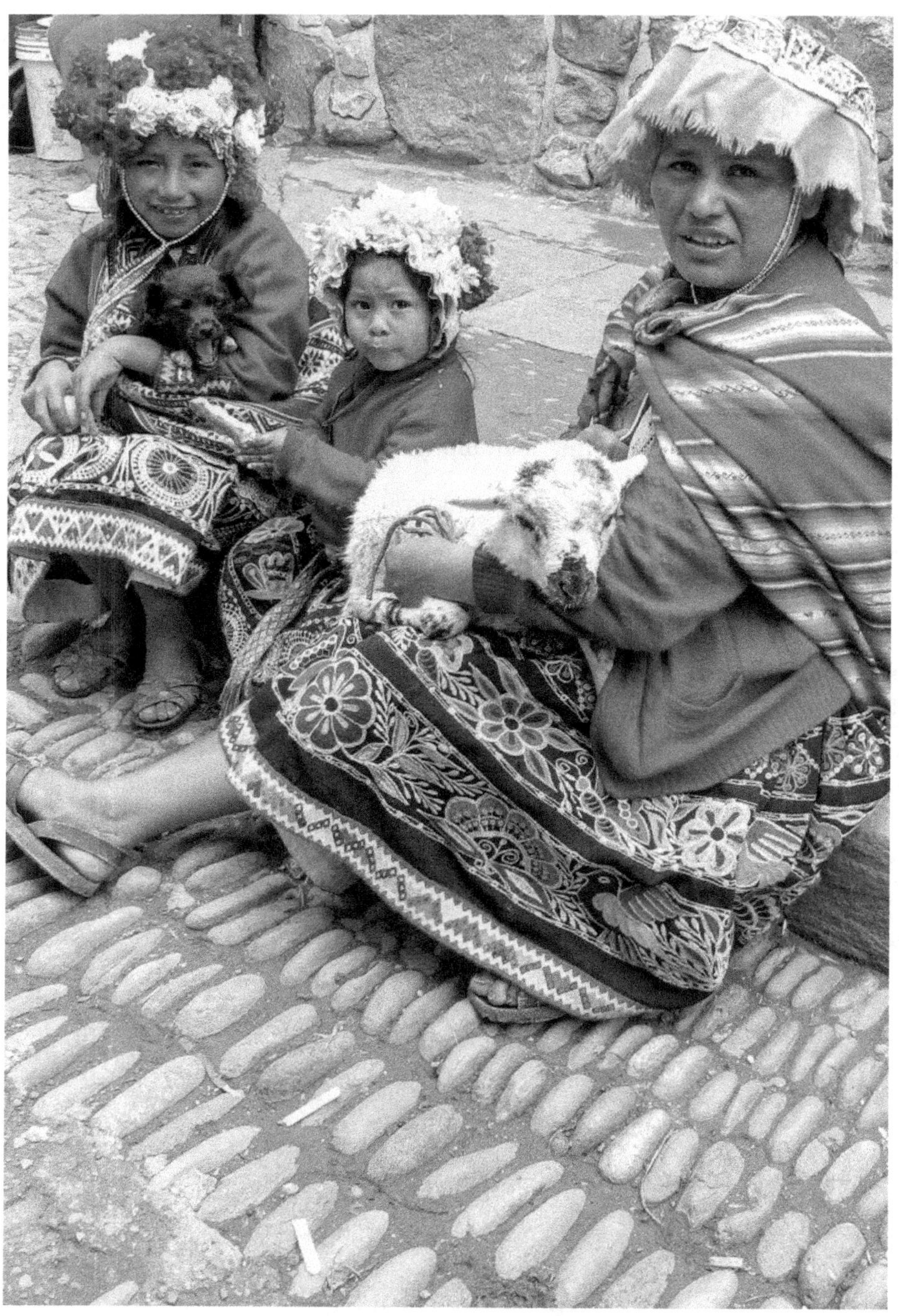

*16. Cusco mothers and daughter, Peru*

The longer you stay in one place, the more opportunities you have to build relationships with the local people, including men. These rewarding friendships help the outsider discover more about the culture.

As a foreigner, your mysterious differences make you enticing to the opposite sex. In parts of Africa and the Far East, relationships settle into more open and relaxed situations, and friendships are easier to form.

Exercise caution with all this attention. In the poorer countries, you may find men trying to establish a relationship just to get a ticket to someplace better. Follow your instincts. A casual situation for you might mean everything to the person with you. Do not forget to practice safe sex. AIDS exists everywhere you travel.

If you do find yourself in an uncomfortable conversation with a man, do not, even for one second, let a man dominate the situation. You hold the reins. Take control and back off. Do not give in to unpleasant characters, just to keep from seeming rude.

If circumstances permit, look the individual in the eye and, with conviction, tell him to go away and start walking. Sometimes you might have to make a scene or even run away.

I had a conversation with a well-dressed man during breakfast at a nice hotel in Santiago, and he asked for my business card. I asked him to wait outside my hotel room, but he followed me inside. After telling me how much my hair looked like Carol King's, he pushed me on the bed and tried to remove my clothing. After two screams, he ran to the elevator. It is critical for women traveling alone to remain on guard.

Never leave spare hotel keys in your hotel room for a thief to steal and use later. Leaving the "Do Not Disturb" sign on the door intimidates potential thieves.

Find and use the room safe if it allows for a personal combination for locking. Assume others have access to safes in your hotel if those safes require keys. Do not leave personal items on a balcony. Most balconies have paths to next-door balconies.

I did not experience life-threatening danger while traveling, but, upon reflection, I have done some stupid things and hope I have learned to observe my surroundings while traveling instead of concentrating only on the newness of it all. One year, I went to Mali and found a guide whom I hired to take me to the Dogon area.

When we got off the bus in some small city close to Mopti, he talked to several people. Two men I thought were friends of the guide walked us to a house in town. They cleared a room for me, showed me a bucket of water on the roof for bathing, and left me to enjoy the unique surroundings.

I saw mud-shaped rooms along corridors on the way up to the roof, and I will never forget the stars in the sky that night. While bathing, I left all my gear in my room without doors. Midnight in an unfamiliar city, the name of which I never found out, brought me into a strange situation full of stares and whispers. I was neither robbed nor harmed physically but could have been and not one person knew where I was.

I never knew if my guide knew these men before our arrival in the city, but he hired them as our cook and porter for our trip the next day. However, after I gave them all my local currency for food for the trip at the market, we never saw them again.

Pay attention to your watch, as well as the night sky. Once, when absorbed in catching up on the internet, I forgot the time.

I came out of the rural China Internet café hidden in the back alleyways of stone steps and closed doorways. I had no flashlight and no memory of how to get to my little guesthouse. A boy found me wandering, took my sweaty hand, and pulled me toward the hotel.

My status as the sole foreigner in the village worked to my advantage because the locals knew my guesthouse location. My guesthouse owner had no idea of where I had gone and if I had not come back where to look for me. The evening might not have ended so perfectly.

Leave plenty of time to catch trains, buses, etc. in case you get lost. Finding your way on your own can cause frustration.

People-watching in a strange city can give you a fresh insight into the culture. If you hide in the interior of a restaurant lit by candlelight, take advantage of your position, and allow yourself to enjoy watching the activity around you. Try to eat before or after the busy dinner hour since you might face rejection in seeking a table if you are alone.

Eating alone calls for embarrassing attention from others. However, it gives you the opportunity to reflect on the day's activities while enjoying your food at your leisure without possible boring conversation. Take advantage of your hotel restaurant if you fear going out at night alone.

Wheeled luggage helps. Your luggage gets heavier as the days go by, as you grow tired of pulling it, and as you keep adding souvenirs to it. It turns into a challenge in subways or the underground where there are so many stairs. On occasion, I let my bag slide down stairs, keeping my hand on the strap and making sure nobody walks below, as it gets moving fast. Going up, I pray for some young man to help me.

Many questions arise as you think about the idea of traveling alone. Are you outgoing or shy?

Can you walk into a bar or restaurant alone and feel comfortable?

Can you make decisions on your own? If you have no transportation, do you have the courage to face the challenge? What would you do if you missed the one plane leaving your town until the next week? Are you strong enough to carry your own luggage? Will solitude please you? Can you follow directions and read maps?

Even if you answered "no," to these questions, I would not suggest that you should avoid traveling alone. I believe you expand into a different person when you travel alone.

You tend to let your hair down. You leave your masks at home. Except for the last couple of questions, even after all my traveling, I would still answer "no" to all of them. However, I have traveled for years alone and love it. My confidence blossoms on trips.

Sitting in a cafe in downtown Bangkok, late at night, a downpour threatened my comfort zone. Waiting for the rain to stop, I realized the streets had started to fill with water.

When I decided to walk to my guesthouse, the water rose to two feet deep and raw sewage, trash, and mud floated in it.

I knew if I got my new boots wet in this kind of humidity, they would stay wet for the next three weeks of my trek into the jungle.

I pleaded with a little man in the restaurant to let me borrow his flip-flops until tomorrow.

He gave in and laughed as I plodded back with justifiable apprehension in the knee-deep liquid.

The black alleyways of a monastery offered a scary shortcut. Cats screamed and caught me off guard, while adrenaline pushed me toward the safety of my home-away-from-home.

Think about the various situations you might encounter abroad and how you would handle them alone. Stay honest with yourself.

Realize that unexpected things will happen when you travel, but if you keep your eyes open, an adventure will transpire. Remember, you have friends all over the world; you just have not met them yet.

Hotel employees, bus drivers, guides, and shop owners are just some of the people who can help you when you are far away from home. No one can deny the romance of travel.

The indulgent freedom of making decisions on where and when without compromise makes traveling alone magnificent.

There are many sites for finding female travel companions and women-only trips. Check out www.journeywomen.com, www.womentravelingtheworld.com, www.callwild.com or www.cruisemates.com.

***COMPANIONS***

Consider the pros of traveling with a companion. When traveling with someone, you share the joys and challenges of the trip. In addition, you share the costs of accommodations, food, taxis, toiletries, and even clothing.

No more self-timed photos or mealtimes with strangers feeling sorry for you. As you compare thoughts from the day's events while sipping tea in the local plaza, opinions and reactions from a different perspective might surprise you. How exciting to hear that your companion photographed that leopard you thought you had missed while fumbling with memory cards in your pack.

A dependable travel companion motivates you, shares your interests, and adds value to your plan, whether it includes museums or narrow alleyways, leading to hidden treasures.

A companion will encourage you to move forward, whereas, when alone, you might decide to write off that afternoon bus trip to the local hot springs for a dip before dinner.

Having a companion offers a security net. Decisions come much easier when two think about the pros and cons of travel options. Sharing food gives you an escape route if one dish tastes awful.

Taking turns while watching luggage or standing in long bus lines gives each a chance to sit for a while or use the toilet.

The hardest part of traveling alone involves getting sick. If you travel with a companion, he or she can pamper you, run to the pharmacy for pain relief, or hike to the market for sodas to settle your stomach problem. They can help carry luggage or make decisions when faced with twenty buses in a parking lot, knowing that only one goes in the right direction, and you want to sit back and close your eyes.

One person might spot danger more quickly than the other can. What you forget, the other person may remember.

Reminders from your friend may make you check for your passport (that you left on your bedside table instead of slipping it into a safe place), or consider how much money to change before the next stop. Unless you laugh at yourself a lot, having a friend helps find the humor in situations that might otherwise be annoying.

Traveling alone makes it impossible to share with another your experiences, as words in postcards just cannot describe the beauty of that purple sunset. Contemplate the cons when traveling with someone you do not know well. If you meet a stranger online, it will be very different traveling with them compared to traveling with a friend.

They might annoy you after days of walking by your side. They might leave you behind or take your money.

Getting the restaurant bill causes all kinds of hassles if one person drinks and the other does not.

Splitting the costs causes embarrassment for the person not drinking, as she feels guilty about saving her money.

Traveling with others makes it much more difficult to meet new people along the way. You end up communicating with each other, so other travelers shy away from invading your privacy by interrupting.

Is your partner a clean freak, or do they leave everything strewn about? Do disagreements over where to go control every conversation? Do you go your own way and meet up again at night?

If so, you might as well travel alone. Putting up with the other in order to make a unanimous decision can lead to frustration.

Traveling with another tests friendships and relationships like nothing else. Consider these issues when traveling with a companion.

Set ground rules before the trip starts.

Find out if your companion snores, and either deal with it with earplugs or find another companion.

Talk about sleep habits like wake-up times, choosing beds, sharing toilets, timing for showers, and allocating counter space. Let your partner know before the trip about potential personality conflicts.

# Chapter 12: people

*"Reinvent yourself by living outside your boundaries for a while."*

***CULTURAL DIFFERENCES***

Foreign travel should take a treasured place as one of the most significant times in your life. In discovering how different people can behave in their dress, food, and attitudes, you will begin to see similarities between them. By getting to know foreigners, we even bridge the gap at home between people in our neighborhoods, churches, and perhaps within our own families between generations.

Despite the bus driver's suggestion that we stay at the bus station until morning, I, and a couple of passengers who had been with me on the New York to Mali flight, decided to take a taxi to find a downtown hotel. On the midnight drive, shadowy figures moved closer to fifty-gallon oil drums filled with flames. Their unsmiling faces were lit by the vivid colors of the fires. "What in the world am I doing here?" I whispered to myself.

Without any signs of regret or fear, the man next to me said, "Aren't they beautiful?"

The black night hiding those haunting faces scared me, and my first thought was, can I deal with being alone with these strange people? But the positive attitude from the passenger on my flight was like a wonderful slap in the face. Of course, I can, and this is why I am here. The chill of the night caused the locals to move outside close to the fire for warmth. What a beautiful sight. Understanding the underlying reasons why events happen when we travel helps smooth the water's edge. You will find diversity of customs, religions, and behaviors. When traveling and in everyday life how we deal with the differences counts. Our unconscious interpretations turn into clouded reactions to the values of our own culture.

One of my teenagers used to laugh at photos of tribal men of New Guinea wearing nothing but penis gourds. In Germany, I often witnessed children drinking wine at the dinner table. In the United States, consider the rules against these practices. By realizing that our culture exists as one of hundreds, we will triumph over our cultural prejudices.

Respect and kindness surpass our inabilities to communicate and understand the differences between ourselves and others. Despite the fact that we can get by without speaking the local language and recognizing customs, we should express a positive and resourceful attitude towards our hosts. Appreciate the differences. Researching the culture before we travel helps to prepare for the strangeness of the new environment. Asking questions and observing local traditions gains us additional respect from the natives. When we see similarities, we need to participate. Global communication has changed our reputation as "The Ugly American." Organizations to save the world educate each of us about the environment and its best resource, the people. We can transform ourselves into citizens of the world.

The experiences we bring home from another culture help us to understand our own world and, most importantly, ourselves. Learning about another culture and making friends in that culture help bridge the gap between our worlds.

### *CULTURE SHOCK*

In time your senses will begin to adjust to a foreign country, but until then, plan on culture shock due to the inability to relate to the new environment. Culture shock involves your inability to connect with reality. Adaptation to a strange culture and climate can cause disorientation in the absence of cues from familiar surroundings. From the moment you step off the plane, you fight the language barrier and the exchange of foreign currency. You stick out like a sore thumb.

The resulting stress will either increase or decrease your interaction within the new habitat. Preventive medicine for this potential dilemma consists of a large dose of studying beforehand the customs of your new environment. The road to help you achieve a better worldview comes from understanding the differences of this new culture. Take the time to acquaint yourself with what happens around you.

The best international flights arrive at night, so you must find a hotel and catch up on needed sleep. If arriving during morning hours, take it easy with a few walks in the neighborhood of your hotel to acclimate to foreign words. Try not to spend the day in bed; otherwise, you will not sleep well at night, and you may have difficulty adapting to the new time zone.

Overexposure, excessive burdens, fearfulness, hassles, extreme climates, and worry can all lead to the anxiety called stress. Stress can exhibit itself in body and mind. Most travel addicts react with a positive attitude toward the changes and uncertainties that await them in foreign lands, an essential part of the adventure. Living out of a suitcase can turn into a demanding and exhaustive chore. Postpone that feeling by staying a few days in one place, unpacking, catching up on laundry, and writing in your journal. The hassles of boys begging for business sometimes outweigh what a place has to offer. Private space, difficult to find, relieves that suffocation, so get to a private place when you can. Dealing with pushy young entrepreneurs day-in and day-out peels away layers of patience.

Culture shock includes the inability to relate to your surroundings. The cultural setting you find yourself in may inhibit adaptation and increase your discomfort. Senses remain on hold for so long, and then we push the fast forward button. Energized by an exotic, strange, or unfamiliar environment, you must use active care to assess the situation. From the minute you step off the plane, you arrive into an arena of hustlers yelling alien words and grabbing for your luggage. You do not get the chance to find your hotel and recover from jet lag. Changing money, finding food that looks edible, along with shelter for the night should rank high on a priority list.

In the beginning, the shock of a foreign environment excites you and keeps you on your toes. Although disoriented by the strangeness, your senses delight in the newness of the unfamiliar. The intrigue causes your sense of curiosity to run wild. You cannot contain the excitement presented by the possibilities that surround you. Motivation from the newness of rituals, food, and the peculiar environment soon turns into fatigue.

For some, it takes days and days before they suffer from constant sensory stimulation. Without immediate acclimation to our new environment, we notice everything, even those things that normally would not bother us. Our tolerance fades and symptoms of irritability, loneliness, sleeplessness, lack of appetite, moodiness, and feelings of helplessness set in. Balancing your perception and attentiveness with the reality of your surroundings challenges the traveler at all times. Culture shock seeps into your days and creates restlessness at night.

The first signs of culture shock, (in addition to the symptoms mentioned above), include a basic irritability with the way locals do things. You lack a feeling of belonging, and wonder whether people care about you. Decisions equal impossibilities, and you think of going home.

The next set of feelings lasts several days. You begin to wonder about yourself, and why you came, as you adjust to the local food, customs, and language. Appreciating this new reality feels like landing on another planet. You isolate yourself, asking why you are here. Finally, you begin to accept the situation and get comfortable. If you stay to face your challenges, you begin to submit to the local customs. You find it hard to agree with the way things happen, but you go along anyway. You function in a normal manner again.

The time you have looked forward to will occur when you have adapted to customs and behaviors, and the local people accept you for yourself. Some trips work out as planned, but during others, you have to make adjustments. Sometimes culture shock forces you to reassess your options. On every trip (except for Mali), I slid into the culture, adapting to it and loving every minute of my newfound space within.

In Mali, I began to dislike the native boys who followed me and ordered fried chicken at my regular hangout, a little restaurant on the River Niger. I had no way to explain to the server that I traveled alone and was not paying for their food. One boy offered to take me to the bank for ten dollars. Noticing my camera, another promised me a wedding ceremony to photograph in a nearby village for one hundred dollars. We negotiated. On the way to the river, he stopped and spent his twenty-dollar payment on a can of salmon and some cigarettes. He ate the fish on the way to the river showing off to his buddies his recent wealth and smoked half the package before reaching the water. Of course, half way through the trip to the village, I realized, in my eagerness to photograph a rare event, I fell for his trickery. He made a false promise of a wedding ceremony when in fact these people did not feel comfortable with a stranger in their village wanting to take photographs. I said he had to figure out a way to allow me to photograph the people of the village living their lives, as an invisible observer. He begged a storeowner for a sack of candy and paid for every picture I took with candy.

An American magazine, *Transitions Abroad*, used one of those village photos for a cover shot, so benefits came from the initial setback. The magazine wanted me to write a story about my experiences, and I tried to explain that being in Mali overwhelmed me.

The constant attention wore me down, and by the middle of my trip, I wondered why I chose to come to Mali. It got to the point where I needed to create diversions, to sever my ties with the Mopti community. Wanting to make their fortune on any tourist walking by, young teenage entrepreneurs hung around every street corner. Since I was the only tourist in town, I felt the constant attention every second I left the safety of my hotel grounds. They would offer to walk me across the street for ten dollars. I took day trips to river villages. Finally, I changed my plans altogether, left for Timbuktu, and had an awesome adventure.

Looking back, I appreciate what I went through in Mali because I will have a higher level of tolerance next time, and it gave me a better understanding of how much patience it can take to adapt to a foreign culture. Plus, the offer to write a story about Mali turned into two paying articles as I did some soul searching for all those little treasures that had become hidden by the overbearing personalities of the men of Mali.

Travelers face culture shock in two ways: Either they give in, leaving their own culture behind, or they withdraw from their new environment. I have met travelers like myself, afraid to leave their hotels, and for days, the gate of their hotel replaces their security blanket until their flight leaves to return home. Intense and constant hassles affect individuals differently.

My more recent travels took me to less-developed areas, which helped me understand the magnitude of change I have to endure. In Bangladesh, the problems that arose constantly frustrated me in ways I had not experienced. My 6:00 a.m. flight from Dhaka to Chittagong was cancelled, and I was to meet my tour guide in Bandarban at 1:00 p.m. the next day. I had to make that bus from Chittagong at 10:00 a.m., or I would miss my trip into the jungle to see the Tripura tribes. I hired a private driver at the airport. We were lost within ten minutes of leaving the airport, but the worst of the tale was the craziness of the drivers on the six-hour trip. At times, there were six vehicles across the two-lane road, all pushing to get their way. Often their vehicles shoved us into the ditch or into the side of a huge bus or dump truck that just simply did not budge. I have never been in such fear of dying as I was on that road.

The best way to deal with the shock of a new culture begins at home with attention to research. Practical tips in guidebooks will help you meet the challenge of your new reality. Carry that guidebook everywhere while abroad. It will save your life.

Your constant patience will pay off enormously. Although you may disagree with the outcome of a decision made by a taxi driver or guide, negative attitudes will never resolve the problems. If you end up in an argument with someone in a different culture, keep in mind maybe they had a bad hair day, so do not judge the entire culture by one episode.

Guidebooks will give you hints on precautions to take. If new at traveling, heed their advice as it can help with the shock of the newness you experience. Walking the streets of Old Delhi, I looked around trying to see past the trash-filled streets for a clean place offering breakfast. The smells turned my stomach, as a fat cow waded through the sewage, hunting for anything to eat. Two ladies, selling food from a cart, pointed to the restaurant that the guidebook recommended. There were no signs, and no customers inside, but the eggs and toast were delicious. I discovered a little gem in the middle of the chaos of Indian life. That encounter turned into a building block, an introduction to the local culture.

The information from books will not tell you everything you need to know to keep culture shock from affecting you. Without a good attitude, respect, and trust, you compromise your ability for cultural acclimation. The best immunization against culture shock involves accepting the diversity of a culture and adapting to it.

### *RESPECT*

Behavioral expectations about people differ from culture to culture. Holding hands in public or exposing any part of a woman's body (except her hands, feet, and face) can cause problems in some countries. Sleeping in a hotel room with a friend of the opposite gender, talking about sex in public, wearing shorts, wearing short skirts, or (as a woman), traveling alone, may be customs we take for granted in the United States.

You may disagree with the caretaker of the mosque who asks you to remove your shoes before you step inside, but that will give him a false impression of Americans, and you will still not get in the door.

Do not alienate yourself from the very people with whom you will live temporarily.

Comments about political issues and government officials qualify as topics to avoid in other countries. In the United States, we can joke about the President, but in foreign countries, avoid the risk of rude behavior. Such language may violate the local law.

In foreign countries, curiosity prevails. You attract the curiosity of locals, and the stares come from every direction. This is a normal reaction to new sights.

Just tell yourself curiosity flows both ways. I believe that phrase, and have no problem bathing in rivers with curious eyes, watching from behind trees upriver. When I live with tribal people who wear no clothing, they have to wonder if my body looks like theirs under all my layers of weird clothing. Out of respect, they hide and watch as I manipulate my sarong while I bathe. Expect unusual questions and looks of, "What's that?"

A Dani woman of New Guinea who shaves her head and plucks all of her body hair may want to touch my long brown hair. A nomad of the Borana tribe of Somalia, wearing a gorgeous sarong and white cloak, wanted to put his fingers in the pockets of my shirt. Keep an open mind and leave your prejudices at home.

Important virtues to remember when traveling include kindness and patience. Your status as the guest while traveling results from your choice to visit that country. By respecting the host, you receive acceptance as an honored guest. You will leave villages with more than gifts of jewelry, hand-woven sarongs, or carved masks. Sharing stories of each other's lives, the goodbye handshakes, and requests for your return will sink deep in your heart.

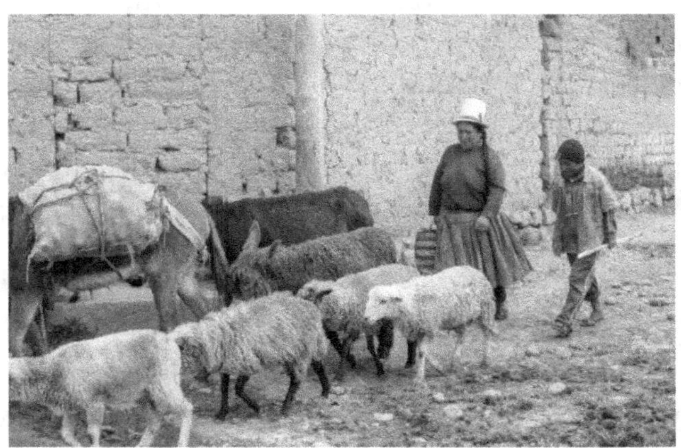

*17. Walking home from salt mines, Peru*

### BRINGING BACK GREAT MOMENTS, DIGITALLY, OR ON FILM

Adventure traveling deserves recording. Will you remember the look on the face of the two-hundred-pound orangutan as he growled at your intrusion? Hearing the laughter of children at home reminds you of the children making mud pies in the sandy streets of Timbuktu. Take lots of pictures.

Thank goodness for the underwater camera. Were those seals or penguins swimming under your legs off the beach in the Galapagos? Memory recalls the struggling rickshaw driver pulling your heavy packs, but did he have bare feet? Dad keeps bragging about climbing up to the Parthenon in Greece. Photos remind you that your youngest fell off a bucking horse in the jungles of Guatemala. Your mind is a junkyard, saving memories of the day the little boy in kindergarten kissed you, but forgetting what your guide looked like on your month-long India journey.

Photography allows you to recall memories of where you traveled and the faces of the people you met. You will not only have something to show your friends and family, but you will have something that helps you re-live the stories in full color, with all the detail, something that will put memory to work again. Photography takes a lot of effort, but years later you will appreciate the time and money you spent taking photos.

Your personal choice of equipment depends on the commitment you make. You will have to consider all the pros and cons of expensive, heavy equipment versus a basic point-and-shoot.

Expensive, professional cameras allow for creativity, adjustments for exposure, and flexibility to deal with the conditions of your day. When out walking, if you see the steeple of a mosque silhouetted by a full moon, do not expect your point and shoot to compete with results offered by an expensive manual camera. When others carry your luggage, they find heavy, fragile lenses a pain to deal with. More than once, I have had lenses dropped by porters who do not understand the meaning of breakable. Take into consideration the weight of your camera bag. My camera weighed four pounds, but with two lenses, a flash, and oodles of film, it ended up close to twenty-five-pounds. Today, digital solves the film problem and lighter designs save weight.

Although you have more control of photograph quality using an expensive camera, consider the disadvantages. Your camera should belong to your body like your money belt. Without it, you should feel naked. Because a heavy camera's size exceeds that of a point and shoot, you will need a special bag for it, in addition to any other daypack you carry. Stores have all kinds of camera packs for the shoulders, or for wearing around your waist, leaving your hands free to photograph.

Thieves target tourists everywhere you go, so do not set the bag or camera down even for an instant without guarding it at every moment. Tourists have lost many a camera by setting it down to put their sunglasses on. Children appear out of nowhere, running past and snatching a bag or camera. Caught off guard, tourists take a few seconds to realize what has happened, and by the time they do, the children have disappeared into alleys and to the safety of the adults who have pushed them into this business.

Take a copy of your camera receipt with you while traveling, to avoid trouble with paying duty while going through customs, especially if your camera came from overseas. Carry your bag in a carry-on for plane travel. Dropped luggage is a common problem when you are relying on baggage handlers, and you might open your bag to a shattered lens. If you deplane on a stopover, take your camera bag with you. Never leave expensive camera equipment in an overhead if you leave the plane. An overhead bin on a plane provides a safe place for a valuable camera bag while using the lavatory but not if on a foreign long-distance bus or train. Keep zippers closed and straps around your neck, not just over your shoulder. Using a plain bag instead of an expensive camera pack will detour potential thieves.

The limitations of a point-and-shoot compared to a heavy film camera will keep you from spending too much time looking through a lens. Often, I look forward to a day without a heavy camera, knowing I want to capture everything I see. That little pocket camera will give you more free time to take in the smells and laughter, and you still have a visual record of your trip. A thief will not grab a camera stuck in your waist pouch or pocket as fast as a separate camera bag. Greater size and expense makes you more vulnerable to thieves.

No matter what camera you use, learn about it before you go. Understand the different functions when using it for landscapes, portraits, people, and flash. Figure out in advance how best to load and unload batteries and memory sticks, so you will not miss that once-in-a-lifetime photo while traveling.

Put new batteries in your flash and camera before you go and take enough batteries to change as needed. Do not count on buying batteries abroad. They cost more. Double A batteries sit on shelves in small shops for years so watch expiration dates if purchasing them.

Some waterproof cameras hang around your neck while you swim with seals or snorkel with sharks. In Puerto Rico, my waterproof camera went crazy shutting on and off after immersion in the water for several hours. The local grocery store had a disposable waterproof camera that at least gave us the memories of kayaking in the ocean while starfish snuggled in the sand below us.

Protecting your equipment from the elements is a challenge if you travel in the rainy season, in the desert, while sailing, or if you travel anywhere that weather or humidity can surprise you. When I travel in desert areas, I wrap a sarong around my camera when it is out of the bag. Never store your camera in plastic, as the condensation can play games with the electronics of your camera. In the jungle of northern Thailand, my video camera stopped working from the humidity. At night, I put the camera in a breeze to help dry it out. The next day I woke up and photographed my most favorite photo, a Karen tribal woman talking to a neighbor.

On another trip, while crossing an algae-coated log bridge in Borneo, I fell in a river with my camera around my neck. My guide grabbed the strap, pulled the camera out in seconds, and proceeded to remove his sarong to wipe the camera. Back in my village hut, I wiped the camera as dry as possible and removed the lens. Next day, the camera worked well.

Bring your camera booklet in case you get in a pinch and cannot figure out a setting, or copy the pages of interest. Technology has given us new video and digital cameras, lightweight and affordable. Think about your itinerary, how you would like to use a camera, and think about batteries. You will have to do some research to know about conversion plugs for your battery charger and suitable voltage to charge it. This information is easy to find online. One set of converter plugs and adapter will cost less than twenty dollars. With the proper adapter, I have found rechargeable batteries perfect for travel.

The advantage of portraying moving images in their natural surroundings with sound can add to the fun of any trip. The temperature- and moisture-sensitive parts cost much to repair and require more babying than a still camera.

Will you want to view the memories of your trip on a computer or television screen? The constant vibrations from bumpy roads to trekking over jungle roots and under vines can wreak havoc with capturing a steady movie. Newer digital equipment can reduce the number of moving parts.

Respect the locals when photographing people and objects. Ask permission to photograph people under all circumstances. In many remote societies, people believe their spirit disappears when you photograph them.

An old Navajo woman told me that she believes people could perform horrible acts on her by using her photograph. She made me promise to share my photographs with caution. In remote areas, people seeing a camera will run away or turn their backs to you. If you ask their permission, they will stand erect and stare into the lens. I pretend to take the photo, say thank you, and wait until they go back to their normal routine. Then I shoot the photo. Most the time it looks like I have joined a movie set, with the local people acting out their day-to-day lives with me.

In touristy areas, tribal people receive pay for photographs of themselves or their belongings, including photographs of the rocks in front of their huts. In this case, do not try to sneak photographs in order to save a few cents. I have done this and been yelled at, pointed at, and mothers have chased me when I have walked past their children carrying a camera. Privacy remains a privilege, even in the smallest corners of the world. People in Muslim countries will exhibit reluctance to pose unless they understand the concept of money (meaning they will pose for money) and adjust their beliefs accordingly.

Before you go to an area, check the local restrictions on photography. You may not have permission to photograph inside churches, monasteries, mosques, the outside of government buildings, bridges, military installations, some historical areas, border crossing areas, air, train and boat facilities, or at and religious ceremonies like funerals. Ask if you are not sure.

Do not forget to take photographs of the friends you make. People pictures will enliven memories much quicker than photos of local monuments. Markets offer many opportunities for photographs, but you will have to ask permission for close-ups. I often fail to get permission to shoot in local markets. Buy some fruit for a snack or spices for a favorite aunt to coax the seller into saying yes to a photo.

Get up before dawn, the time when the villagers greet the day with routine chores, chatting with neighbors, taking care of animals, while their children run and laugh. Some places inspire awe at sunrise. The spiritual light of a sunrise enhances any photo opportunity, whether it is of the face of a child anxious for breakfast or whether it is the Golden Palace of Bangkok.

Whether in downtown Calcutta, or deep in the jungles of Peru, get out and walk. You will have a better sense of the culture. Talk to people along the way, and in their language, if you know a few words. You might find yourself surrounded by locals. Do not let this intimidate you. They like to see the strangeness of your clothing or your pack. Kindness and respect will lead to a conversation including an invitation for a meal or tea. Quite often, you will run into the same travelers you met the week before. You either use the same guidebook or have similar tastes. Undoubtedly, the longest lasting memories will focus on the friends you meet along the way. Find out about ceremonies or festivals coming up in the area you plan to visit so you can plan to be there and take photographs. You can find out about festivals and other activities from local guides. You might discover the most incredible adventure you can imagine.

While trekking deep in the heart of New Guinea, I wandered into three separate festivals, all different and unique. One had over two thousand natives most of whom had never seen white skin before. For several days they gathered, walking for miles to participate in pretend war battles and dancing all night. My teenage daughter Katherine and I joined in midnight dances and once were caught in the middle of a war battle with shooting arrows that turned out to be plant stems.

While traveling, stay cautious and courteous, but above all, remain adventurous. Even though you have a fear of heights, you might find a situation where the one way out leads up as I experienced in Mali visiting the Dogan people. The all-day climb straight up a 200-foot escarpment still gives me chills when I think about it. A tiny spring loosened gravel enough to make me slip and lose my footing and eyeglasses. However, my fondest image of Mali includes the view of the village at the top of that cliff. The people, the food, and my room all come back to haunt me like a friendly ghost. I can still hear the strips of hand-woven cotton hung over the doorways and calling my name in the wind. The challenge I met that day returned extraordinary rewards.

### *SCRAPBOOK MEMORIES*

You will run across all kinds of things to put in a scrapbook or add to your photo album as reminders of a special place. Postcards do not cost much and are available everywhere. They help preserve memories, and they provide a backup if your photograph of a remarkable place did not turn out. Matchbook covers, paper menus, coasters, maps, transportation ticket stubs, dried flowers, or leaves all make suitable mementos. In Irian Jaya, while climbing a steep and slippery path beside a trickle of water, my young guide stopped and picked a leaf to wipe across my forehead to cool me. The humidity had weakened me, and the leaf felt cool and wet. I called the leaf the "air conditioning plant" but never could interpret his name for the plant. I wish now I had one of those leaves for my journal.

### *JOURNALING*

Like a scientist, we take notes to access the past and to recapture faded memories.

As with a photograph album, our field notes satisfy our hunger for travel with memories of days gone by. Unlike a photograph album, a journal gives us the opportunity to vocalize in writing all the difficulties of a situation. Your senses can play in your journal, divulging all their secrets.

A photograph can remind you how something looked. Your journal helps you recall the incredible smells in the markets of Cuzco or the sounds of the constant laughter of children, playing along the water's edge of the Amazon. These things could disappear from your consciousness forever, so write them down.

Communicating with pen and paper, you can confess your true feelings about situations, people, or even hassles. Written reflections help you retain memories for personal growth later.

By writing about your attitudes, you may unearth some significant self-revelations. For example, you may not realize how much you depend on people in your life until you spend time alone.

The routines of your life might appear quite normal until you change them and eliminate the boredom.

Traveling may reveal your need for less socializing and drinking. You might also discover physically that you feel better if you walk a few miles every day.

Journals reveal much about a person, which distinguishes the journal from a photographic record of events. Challenges you faced, and how you handled yourself, make exciting entries.

In describing the essence of things, you trap experiences on paper. Dreams, fantasies, passions, and intense situations crawl across the page, described in details that only you would read. In trying to report the individual sounds of a jungle, you learn to listen carefully.

Painting an accurate picture of a local market, remembering crafts, traditional dress, and foods for sale require careful observation. You do not need training as a professional journalist to express the sights, sounds, and tastes, but you can return to those places at any time if you journal. After your memories start to fade, as home commitments begin to take priority, the value of these notes and images weighs heavy on your heart.

Jotting down your feelings about life, you begin to see a new perspective of things. Without all the materialistic things, your job and relationships missing, you can write about all that you appreciate. Soon you will begin to see that significant things must take priority when you return home, like exercising more often or eating a different diet.

Maybe not all those deserts are necessary every night. A journal has many benefits, but the best reward comes from getting to know yourself a little better.

### *TAPE OR AUDIO RECORDERS*

Remember sounds by recording them on a small audio recorder. Years later, you can recall many incredible events just by listening to the sounds of your boat, conversations with new acquaintances, or traditional instruments, driving dancers wild. Use a recorder to remember a guide's description of a place or a local person telling you a folktale.

In Ubud, Bali, I discovered the son of Gusti Lempad, living in his father's home. Lempad died at 116 in 1978, and many believe he helped establish the world's respect for Balinese art. Interviewing his son gave me closeness to the culture.

A funny thing happened one night deep in the virgin jungles of Ethiopia. After dark, I turned on my tape recorder to capture the incredible sounds of baboons, playing in our campsite; monkeys, jabbering in the trees; and an occasional growl of something big. A few hours later, I heard an unfamiliar clicking sound. I had hired a young boy with a machine gun to circle my tent for the night because of the active tribal warfare. One tribe accused another tribe of killing a lion that belonged to them. The boy walked back and forth nervously, pacing around my tent with his gun all night. Through the fabric of the tent, I saw different parts of the jungle light up when he used my flashlight. I figured the constant clicking sounds came from natives, signaling each other in the bush. I listened for hours until daylight. When I sat up, I realized the clicking noise came from my tape recorder, which had run out of tape and circled round and round, waiting for attention. I did not get any sleep that night, as I lay motionless in the intense heat, imagining painted faces slashing my tent and seeing my white, sweaty body, quivering in the dark.

Squeals sounding on the tape from baboons having fun in our campsite help me to recall that night, which otherwise might disappear from my treasure chest of experiences.

# Chapter 13: traveling with children

*"Our greatest natural resource is the minds of our children."* Walt Disney

### *PATIENCE*

Barrels of patience: a must for traveling with children. Things never go as planned, and a well-thought-out second plan helps relieve stress for both parents and children. Lower your expectations and remind yourself that children can have bad days. Children do not understand that vacation calls for your best behavior in spite of the absence of favorite toys, foods, and comfy beds that surround them at home.

### *SLEEP*

Make sure your entire party begins a trip with plenty of rest. Remember to reserve cribs or extra beds in the hotels at your destination before leaving home. This will assure you of comfortable places for the children to rest at naptime.

Check, if you are staying with relatives, about sleeping arrangements to give them a heads up as to what you need to make your children as comfortable as possible. Maybe they can borrow portable cribs if needed. Keep children on their normal sleep schedule. Getting plenty of sleep far outweighs missing a party or outing. Arrange flights during sleeping hours. Overnight international flights allow the whole family to arrive fresh and prepared for their new adventure. Take advantage of stopovers and flight departure delays by using up all that kid energy and encouraging more sleep time. We all tend to lose sleep in strange beds. Instead of moving around from friend to friend or city to city, while traveling, consider staying in one place for a few days.

### *FLYING*

When making flight reservations, order children's meals for those long flights.

Help young children understand this new adventure. Families complain about airlines splitting them up and letting a young child sit in a middle seat between strangers.

Some airlines are charging for reserved-seat assignments to alleviate the problem of not sitting together. Check-in exactly twenty-four hours before flight time to help guarantee seat preferences. Do not go to an airport without reserved seats.

Call the airlines and talk them into giving you reserved seats if they do not have assigned seats.

A couple of airlines do not allow online reservations for a child under two, flying free. You must call and get an agent to add a lap child.

One airline requires you to go to the airport on the day of your flight with the child's birth certificate to verify the child's birth date. Some airplane configurations do not have extra oxygen masks for use by a lap child, which means splitting up the family and moving members to different rows. Check www.seatguru.com for information about location of oxygen masks.

Car seats have to have a label attached that says FAA approved and many gate agents will check for this label.

There is now a CARES harness that eliminates carrying the heavy car seat but does require the child to have his own seat. The Child Aviation Restraint System is from Kids Fly Safe. It is designed specifically for airplanes and certified by all US Carriers. It can be purchased or rented from Little Traveler Equipment rental for children.

Some airlines have removed microwaves since many do not serve hot foods any longer, but hostesses are willing to warm baby bottles with hot water. Wide-body jets still have diaper-changing areas.

Malaysia Airlines no longer allows babies in first class cabins on some flights due to passenger complaints of babies crying. Bulkhead seats are now reserved for the disabled.

Boarding remains the most common hassle for parents. Frequent flyers and first-class get to board first with most airlines, so families carrying diaper bags, toys, car seats and toys clog the aisles and delay general boarding. Airlines are tightening restrictions for waiving of fees for car seats and strollers. Jogging strollers, non-collapsible strollers, or strollers heavier than twenty pounds are not allowed on some airlines, such as American Airlines.

At gate check-ins, United Airlines bans strollers if they do not collapse. Diaper bags do not count against carry-on limits on some carriers, so check before you go and check on the limitations of the number of free car seats or strollers allowed. Lap children usually do not get any free baggage allowance, so bags will count against the parent carrying them.

If an infant turns two while traveling, United requires a return ticket purchased for the now two-year-old child for the return trip home. TSA rules have changed, concerning children. Children may leave their shoes on, and pat-down procedures are minimal. All equipment must go through metal detection. Baby formula and breast milk, juice and medications, are exempt from the 3.4-ounce limit in reasonable quantities and are specially scanned separately. Pack plenty of healthful snacks. At first, giving a child candy seems to have a calming effect, but it can create hyperactivity or even tantrums. Check to see if your airport or connecting airports have a playground for children. Use up your child's energy with walks before boarding or find an unused gate area for some active playtime with an inflatable beach ball to toss and catch.

While flying, walk up and down the aisles when little ones get active. Consider other passengers when handing your children toys. Pretend cell phones that ring, favorite stuffed puppies playing music, or a portable DVD player boasting hundreds of cartoons without headphones can get annoying to fellow passengers, trying to read or sleep. Bring a few favorite quiet play toys (like activity books and small travel-sized games, available at any toy store). Have a surprise bag that mom alone can dig into and fill it with new toys from the dollar store. Use it as a distraction when your child gets antsy. Look for small containers of Play Dough, books to read, a new container of markers, and a coloring or activity book. For one dollar each, find all kinds of little surprises. Use the toilet often when the seatbelt sign turns off to prevent accidents.

Bring an extra outfit just in case. If traveling with an infant, bring baby wipes and an extra outfit for mom. Some diapers do not do their job, and babies have a tendency to spit up. Plan for delays by having extra snacks and baby formula handy. Arrive well in advance for flights and plan for plenty of time to change planes on stopovers. Chewing gum or sucking on a bottle or breast helps equalize pressure in ears. Change travel plans if your child has an ear infection or cold. Patience and a positive attitude will help steady any turbulence.

### *CARS*

If a drive takes ten hours, plan for twelve. Build in lots of rest stops for your children so that they can release some of that youthful energy. Let the kids run and kick a ball around. Any engaging activity that distracts children from realizing they must stay buckled in a car seat for hours on end will repay you for every extra bag packed.

Keep food routines and sleep habits as normal as possible. DVDs, iPods, laptops, Nintendo DS, and iPads all offer the opportunity to load up on games and movies for hours of entertainment.

Set aside some new movies or games or hide the DS for a few weeks before departure so that the unfamiliar games will take on a fresh new look.

Let each child pack his own backpack of favorite toys and books. Encourage them to participate in the adventure with ideas of what to do while traveling to help pass the time.

Find car games online, such as the license plate game, Twenty Questions, and memory games. Check online at places like www.funandgames.org for hundreds of ideas.

### *GETTING LOST*

Visit online sites for help with prevention of loss, recovery of lost children, and ways to help identify children if they do get lost. Go over rules and teach children the importance of holding hands and not running away to see a cartoon character walking toward them in a crowded amusement park. While visiting a Disney park this summer, my seven-year-old grandson ran ahead and disappeared in the thick crowd of children all wanting to arrive first in line to shoot the water guns at unsuspecting adults below. He was gone for ten minutes or more, and all I could think of was how to find him and explaining to his mom, now back from a toilet break, how a normal day had turned into such a horror. Invest in a wristband for your child or at the very least, attach a nametag with your cell phone number to the inside of his shorts pocket.

Our first Mexican family trip consisted of a three, seven, and ten-year-old with two parents experiencing, what we later called the "train trip from hell." Not allowed to use that "h" word at home, the kids had a reason to share the story often. We had paid for a first- class, air-conditioned room out of Nogales, which had room for four to sleep. But, the room we were led to and told to stay in had one long bench, a toilet full of raw sewage, and no opening window; the air conditioner was not on and the heat felt intense. Thinking we could eat on the train, I brought one package of Ritz crackers. Mostly we would be sleeping, as the trip was only eighteen hours. The filthy, dirty train offered no hope of food or even bottled water. There were uniformed police, walking the train, and they did a great job of keeping us out of the empty rooms that had air conditioning for some reason. We offered them any amount of money to let us have one of those rooms, but they refused and led us back to that horrible room. We spent most of the hours standing between rail cars at the open doorways in the wind.

Surviving the train ride, we found local buses and a little hitching in the back of pickups all the way to Mazatlan, where our children made their first attempt at parasailing; then we traveled to the border via the mangrove swamps of San Blas. The children had fun climbing the Indian ruins of Pacquime in Chihuahua, Mexico. Their best story gave details about mom trying to sneak a small baby iguana into the states through the border. We kept that silly lizard alive for two weeks in a coke bottle, feeding him bugs while we traveled. When we got home and built him a splendid cage, full of expensive synthetic rocks to climb and hide in, he decided to die. Immunizations behind them, the kids could not wait until the next trip, which began better than the first. Communication problems slapped us in the face the first night after a long bus journey up to Lake Atitlan, Guatemala. Not prepared for Spanish menus, I could not decide on any food that the children might eat. The safest food we could eat included toast, spread with refried beans, so we ate that while their father looked for a room spacious enough for a family of five people.

The first argument started when the kids saw three beds and one hammock. Later, one child (the one who picked the longest straw) swung so high he was able to touch opposite walls, swinging over all three beds. Beans on toast, tortillas, or scrambled eggs filled their tummies, and never once did we have a complaint about the food or lack of cold sodas. Not knowing any better, we added chlorine to a gallon jug of tap water, our community-drinking cup. Looking back, I think there were easier ways to purify our drinking water, but that method worked fine. Being one of those well-prepared moms, I had one bag full of art supplies and toys. Micro machines (half-inch-long miniature cars like Hot Wheels) kept Allie, the four-year-old, and Brennan, the eight-year-old, busy for hours and hours. They built towns, roads, and even the ruins of Tikal after climbing them one day.

The older daughter, Katherine, loved art and reading but also tried to get involved with her father in taking some Spanish lessons while we lived with a Spanish-speaking family a few days. While walking through a village or riding in the back of a truck to a market, we made up songs or played guessing games. Each of us bonded with other family members in ways that surprised us. We had to rely on each other for entertainment, safety, finding safe food, and shelter. At home, parents took care of those things. While traveling, the sisters, listening when big brother had an idea of where to go, caught my attention. On that trip, the children gained respect for each other and for their parents, who spent a lot of time behind the scenes at home managing. Children wear psychological masks at home, pretending to like someone in school to gain popularity, or dressing like other children to avoid looking different. We all saw each other in a different light on that trip. The false layers peeled away, and we could sing or dance or act goofy and so what? Nobody judged us. We did foolish things that friends would criticize. One day, in our little rented VW bug, my son Brennan and I drove to Chichicastenango (a delightful market town) for more bargaining. He had learned to bargain and wanted more. On the drive, we picked up two young boys hitchhiking, and we had a tremendous time trying to communicate with them during the drive.

A boat ride on Lake Atitlan the next day took us to a small village to explore. The dirt floor of a windowless hut made a pleasant place to sit while local women took advantage of us three gals and our long hair. They laced handwoven sashes in and out of our hair, tying them up on our heads, knowing that once they tied them up we would love it and offer them money for the pampering.

I will never forget my friend Linda asking me a simple question when we returned. "Why in the world would any parent want to be locked up with her kids in the same room night after night and day after day for over two weeks?" I remember looking at Linda and thinking I had no way to explain to her what happened between our children and us parents for that period. With a little planning on my part to make sure the children had activities to keep them busy, food to give them energy, and lots of rest to greet the next day, how could we not have enjoyed our time together as a family?

# Chapter 14: senior travel

*"He who does not travel does not know the value of men."* Moorish proverb

### *WHAT IS A VACATION?*

Decades ago, the word "vacation" conjured images of beaches and quiet island resorts. Travelers today look for more substance for their time and money, and this includes those people retired from jobs, but not retired from life. Volunteering to help save the turtles, renewing your spirit with meditation, learning about village life, trekking northern Thailand jungles, biking the countryside of Ireland, and sailing the islands of Greece help us feel young and alive.

### *CHANGES IN TRAVEL METHODS*

Whether we are experienced travelers or newbies, age changes the methods of travel we choose, calling for awareness. Five years ago, I chose to sit on a wood saddle for days in the desert on a camel. Sitting on the floor of a dugout canoe with crossed legs meant nothing to my knees. After six hours of not moving, though, they finally went numb. One bowl of rice a day satisfied my appetite while trekking the New Guinea jungles years ago. A month in remote Ethiopia without communication back home gave me time to get to know myself and my real capabilities for survival.

In today's world, neither my body nor my mind wants to deal with those issues. Sure, if a friend came along and pleaded for my company on a trip to small villages in Burma, knowing I would sleep on rock-hard bamboo at night and paddle tiny streams to visit "unknown on any map" villages, I would scream, "Of course, let's go!" However, after passing sixty years of age, I admitted to myself that clean sheets and a fan (versus a hammock with biting bugs) gives me a more restful night's sleep. I would like to continue to call myself an adventurer, or gutsy woman, as many call me, but I guess I have slowed down and look for adventure in less aggressive, hard-to-reach places. Instead of the treat of booking the comfortable hotel for some nights after landing and before departing, but choosing a hut for adventure in between, I can now admit to staying at the hotel more nights and doing adventure travel as day trips.

***PHYSICAL CHANGES***

We all (seniors) think of ourselves as people in our fifties, until we get a glimpse in the mirror. One of the greatest changes I have noticed about friends, travel companions, and myself concerns memory. Lapses of memory are part of the aging process. Preparing ahead of time can keep them to a minimum.

After locking my keys in the car, I made a duplicate set of car and house keys and hid a set in my yard, knowing a taxi or friend could get me home if I lost my keys, and the hidden set would get me into my house. I never lock my door without checking inside my purse for my keys. While traveling, you pull out your keys, unlock your bag to grab a last-minute item, and leave the keys on top of the pile of clothes. The taxi honks, you grab your jacket, zip your bag, and attach the lock hanging open in the zipper pull. Whoops, you just locked the key inside. My last trip, I decided to leave the key in the lock, but, more than once, I found the key hanging from the open lock at the next destination. Toward the end of the trip, I decided to leave the keys safety-pinned to the inside of my waist pouch, creating a new step in unlocking bags. Now I always have to bend over so that the waist bag can reach the locks. Buy locks with duplicate or master keys for all locks. Keep one set in a carry-on bag.

Even twenty years ago, I did not climb to the top of the ruins of Tikal, with my children racing ahead. Bouncing on a camel's wood saddle until nightfall in northern Kenya or trudging through a foot of sand in the Sahara never slowed me down. However, the thought of sitting on that camel for more than an hour or walking that desert without water or shade for eight does not interest me these days.

Consider your energy levels and design trips around those levels. In rural China, I heard about an interesting waterfall, hours from the village. Instead of hiking up over the mountainous, rocky shortcut, I opted for the path connecting villages and rice terraces, and came out at the bottom instead of the top. It was the same waterfall, but twice the distance and time. Wrinkled women sat picking roots along the path's stream, pointing at me with loud words that sounded like, "Go away, this area is ours." My appearance scared them, but I gave them smiles anyway. I carried protein bars, water, sunscreen, and a camera for a day that ended in a rice field with a group harvesting rice. I stepped into their field, hoping they would allow photographs. I pointed to the camera. The old man waved his palm back and forth and went back to cutting and stacking the golden stalks.

Allow time for slowing down, which means extra bathroom stops, if that's an issue for you. Luggage with wheels, packed light, relieves the strain you'll feel from hauling it down long airport and train corridors and lifting it in and out of buses.

Think of stairs in subways and hotels without elevators, and your ability to carry luggage up and down. Folks may open doors and help with luggage if they see a woman struggling with those things, but they might forget that older men need assistance as well.

As we age, the eardrums thicken, making hearing more difficult. If difficulty with hearing affects you, look for printed matter like maps, guidebooks, and written instructions on how to find a recommended restaurant. Our physical activity and weight affect our metabolism. Reducing levels of physical activity changes the number of calories needed by the body's organs like the heart.

Using fewer of the body's muscles contributes to the decline in muscle mass. Fewer calories maintain the same weight from previous years, which means the slowing of our metabolic rate will cause weight gain without proper exercise and reduction of calories. Protein bars answer the problem of finding hearty snacks while on the back roads of your life. Dr. Atkins and Kashi are two brands found in discount and regular grocery stores for less than a dollar a bar. Providing about six grams of protein, they will not fill you up but will satisfy hunger for a few hours.

Look in health food stores like GNC for a huge selection of bars, averaging up to fifty grams of protein per bar. As soon as I find one I like, by the next year, another variety takes its place. If I find a bar I like, I buy a case or two online and keep them in my freezer, ready for the next trip.

When traveling abroad, my obsession for healthful food stays at home. Fresh salads on menus welcome travelers in expensive foreign hotel restaurants. Cities that cater to tourists have plenty of food places with safe and fresh food.

Off-the-beaten-track cafes for tourists offer little opportunity for eating safe raw vegetables and uncooked foods. Find a suitable alternative to keeping regular. Some laxatives cause bloating and gas. Experiment before traveling with tablet forms instead of those mixed with a whole glass of water. Use probiotics in tablet form but try them out before you leave home.

Check into both of the following:

www.roadscholar.org, www.seniortours.com, and also look at www.eldertreks.com, www.cruiseforseniors.com.

Senior travel sites offer active travel tours like walking and all kinds of sports, including snowmobiling.

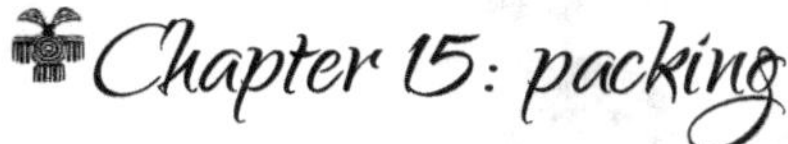

# Chapter 15: packing

*"In every parting, there is a latent germ of madness."* Goethe, 1788

### *PACKING IDEAS*

The more you travel, the less you pack.

Do you dread packing, so you wait until the last minute, and then you throw everything you think you might need into a suitcase? Join the club of thousands who worry about what to take. Forgetting one little item, like a water purifier or your malaria tablets, can ruin your trip. Even seasoned travelers worry about having the right stuff. Having a flexible packing plan allows for packing in the most efficient manner. While finalizing the decision for where and when to travel, start a checklist with categories like what to do before leaving and when returning, what to buy, and what to pack. Don't smother yourself with last minute errands, phone calls to say goodbye, hold mail cards to fill out, clothes to wash, refrigerators to empty, and finding a piece of luggage large enough for your mammoth pile of stuff. Start thinking about your routine chores and what you cannot live without like that favorite album that needs downloading on your iPod or thumb drive. Crossing off that last chore of turning the water heater off as you walk out the door reduces the stress of the adventure.

Some trips call for business or formal attire and others more outdoorsy gear for camping or just beachwear. The basics will stay the same for all types of trips with a few changes here and there. Find the balance. Make a calendar of detailed activities and the types of clothing needed. Do not pack anything not worn at least twice. Try to mix and match all clothing to wear with other articles.

I pack everything in gallon-size Ziploc bags. Intimates and pajamas go in one bag. I divide all other clothing into pants and tops, and each piece is rolled to prevent wrinkles. I wrap shoes in cheap grocery plastic bags, and two extra gallon-sized bags give me a place for wet clothing from rain or swimming, as well as for dirty clothes.

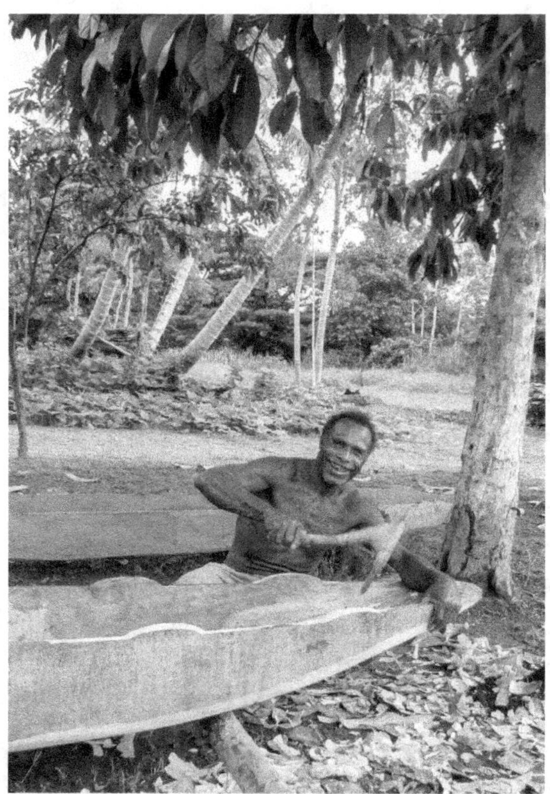

*18. Carving a dugout canoe, Papua New Guinea*

I put all toiletries into Ziplocs, not cute cosmetic bags which take up space. Seeing where the toothpaste is in a kerosene-lit room is a plus. Put your toothbrush in a travel container designed for that purpose for an extra measure of cleanliness.

Keep insect repellents in their own little Ziplocs in case they leak. Ziploc bags are a traveler's perfect answer to an organized packing method.

A few days before leaving, check your bags to make sure you did not forget anything. Consider leaving things behind. Carry your luggage to the door, carry it back again, and ask yourself if it feels too heavy to manage. Remember the height of those over-the-head luggage racks. Will your luggage fit in that space as packed?

If traveling on a budget, then porters will not be carrying your luggage for you. You will handle your luggage yourself. Solo travel means managing those bags in and out of buses, across steep walkways to guesthouses, and in and out of canoes on small Amazon tributaries.

### *TYPES OF LUGGAGE*

Hard-sided luggage with combination locks, although cumbersome and heavy, offers the most security. When you check your bag, prepare to risk loss, delay, or theft of its contents. The number of items stolen from checked luggage after it leaves your hands at the ticket counter has increased over the years, so get luggage that locks.

For me weight scores highest on my list of factors for choosing luggage. Color, fabric, and unusual pockets rank lower. The length of your trip and where you visit do not change the fact that luggage gets heavier with each passing day. No matter what travel you do, first-class to camping, you will tire from hauling luggage around.

Buying a new bag? Then do not consider anything without wheels unless you want to improve your physical shape while you travel. In many airports in the world, you change terminals between domestic and international flights, or at least you have a long walk. Luggage carts offer an alternative if you love your present wheel-less bag.

Soft-sided, molded, or duffel-style luggage (with those essential wheels) work well for most trips. If you purchase nothing else, you will appreciate more and more your investment in a durable, washable canvas bag.

Some bags have another incredible feature, a day bag zippered onto the outside front. This extra bag has many uses. Use it for short jaunts filled only with the items you'll use that day: sunscreen, camera, notepad, maps, glasses, snacks, hat, water bottle, book for waiting in lines, and extra space for those "can't live withouts" you purchase. That quick over-night or extended-day trip calls for a bag with a change of clothing.

In addition, unless you have extra garbage bags, you will appreciate a place to store wet boots or sandy flip-flops after a day of testing your balance on slippery rocks or crossing a muddy stream.

On your return back home, use your day bag for those one-of-a-kind treasures to carry on the plane. If nothing else, use the bag for dirty laundry. Hotel sinks do not exist if you rough it and need to wash in brown, muddy rivers. Check out the bags in the Travel Smith, Magellan, CampMor, or Sierra Trading Post catalogs mentioned in the appendix.

Watch those straps. Straps catch on conveyor belts in airports. They get caught and rip open. All kinds of covers exist for packs, or you can have one made. They look like a giant pillowcase, protecting all those straps, keeping the pack clean, and thieves will not steal a giant blue pillowcase. That brand-new $300 Eagle Creek convertible backpack with wheels looks awesome and fetches double that on the black market. With a cover, your pack does not stand out as one of a rich tourist when tied to the top of a bus.

Make sure your bag has substantial zippers. In addition, look for bags with zippers from either end of the opening. That way, when you close the bag, the two zippers meet, and you can put a small lock through the two loops of the zippers to help frustrate a thief in a hurry. Travel stores and luggage departments in discount houses sell a strap to wrap around your luggage and through handles. To get in the luggage, thieves have to cut the strap, so you will know when you retrieve your luggage if it experienced damage or loss. You can also buy cable-ties or zip-ties at a hardware store, but take a fingernail clipper with you to clip the ties off when you need to get in the bag. Keep that clipper in a carry-on where it is handy. I lock all bags (even carry-ons) out of habit. Local buses in foreign countries put all your bags on the roof with a boy sitting up there sometimes, watching over them. A visible lock or cable-tie deters the boys' curious fingers.

Never put anything in outside zippered compartments if not locked when checking baggage. At San Francisco, waiting to make a claim for my lost luggage, I saw the couple in front of me making a claim. They had their zippered daypack removed from their checked bag, and, of course they had lost all their precious souvenirs which were tucked away inside. It never dawned on them to figure out a way to lock that part of their bag to the larger piece.

Make sure every zipper has locks. If necessary, buy the two-foot long cable from a hardware store that joins with clips and winds through all zipper pulls. This will also serve to lock your bag to the leg of your seat on a bus or open-compartment train.

Buy approved locks in hardware, discount, and travel stores that TSA can access with their keys, and, after checking your luggage, they can lock up again. If TSA goes through your checked luggage, they will leave a card explaining that they searched your bag.

With all the security measures now taken, some airports x-ray luggage right after the check-in at the ticket counter. Passengers can lock their luggage after that x-ray, if they ask to stay and watch their luggage go through x-ray.

For international flights, I always lock my bag. Always. If you carry a knife, or any item that looks suspicious, then your lock might be broken by TSA, so do not pack anything unusual like cans of spray insect repellent or propane for that little cooking stove.

Using a seam sealant from a camping store to waterproof your bag and all seams will save all the items inside if you encounter a downpour. Downpours happen often if you travel during off-season. You will be glad you waterproofed your bag when it lands in a mud puddle.

### *LOST LUGGAGE*

More and more people choose to avoid checking any bags. With airlines handling hundreds of millions of pieces of luggage per year, we hear that tens of thousands of those, or one percent of those checked, never arrive home.

Where do all those lost bags end up? Scottsboro, Alabama now owns the title of the lost luggage capital of the world.

The Unclaimed Baggage Center sells the contents of misplaced and lost bags. They have a staff of appraisers who determine the original value of jewelry, art, clothing, and luggage, and then deduct a set discount. The Baggage Center hosts over 800,000 visitors a year who love the bargains and the entertainment of peeking into what others pack in their luggage.

Why do bags get lost?

The airlines claim late check-in and connecting flights as the main reasons. Bags tagged wrong end up at the wrong destination, or tags get ripped off and, without identification outside or inside the bag, sit for ninety days waiting for declaration of "lost." At times, bags disappear, so keeping valuables in carry-ons keeps you from losing your valuables.

The airlines have different types of compensation for lost luggage with some offering twenty-five dollars to replace incidentals like toiletries. Read the small print when making a reservation for individual airline rules. International rules state the airline will, assuming the passenger used the full limit, pay nine dollars a pound for lost luggage. The airlines and travel insurance offer excess valuation for better protection.

### *CARRY-ON LUGGAGE*

I can squish a month's necessities into a standard carry-on. They start at $30 at the discount stores. Most airlines designate 24"X14"X10" as their maximum carry-on size, with a purse, computer, or briefcase in addition. Fear of losing luggage drives many passengers to carry on their belongings. Avoiding the wait at the carousels for luggage rewards the carry-on fan, alleviating at least one frustration after arriving at an airport and trying to figure out where you need to go and how to get there.

Something else to consider when deciding whether to include a carry-on is the type of travel you do. If you need to keep track of your own luggage, the idea of two or more bags overwhelms.

Most airlines in the United States charge for checked luggage but I have never paid for checked luggage on a foreign airline. Managing luggage without the help of others helps retain sanity during travel to undeveloped areas. We take for granted the train conductor, taxi driver, or airport porters who will help handle our bags here in the United States.

Once you leave the comforts of home, prepare to fend for yourself. If you have a lightweight bag on wheels, the problem disappears.

Carry-on bags work for all kinds of trips: formal, business, beach-types, and camping. One needs to readjust his/her packing procedures to accommodate for the kind of trip planned.

Cumbersome cold-weather down jackets and boots or camping gear can take up too much room for carry-ons.

Several formals or tuxedos and business suits along with several pairs of shoes and accessories can eat up space. Children and babies need care equipment that requires checking. Carry-on luggage simplifies your life when you can arrange it.

Make sure your carry-on has wheels that will stand up to any situation like rolling through sand or on cobblestone walkways. Walk around at home, pulling it to make sure the handle is the proper height. I have pulled bags for what seemed like miles because their handles were too short, and I could not stand up straight.

Figure out a way to put your smaller backpack or under-seat bag onto the wheeled bag for long walks through airports. Hold onto the top strap of your backpack at the same time you are grasping the wheeled bag handle with the second bag sitting on top the wheeled bag.

Packing your carry-on takes thought if you also check another piece of luggage. If your checked piece is lost or misplaced, you want your essential items with you. Think about what you cannot live without and put it in the carry-on. First on that list are comfortable shoes. Packing lists will suggest wearing heavy bulky hiking boots. But logic says that at some point they will have to find a place in your luggage, so you might as well make room for them now and wear or carry on your most comfortable pair of shoes.

Each airline sets limitations on the weight, size, and number of bags passengers check or carry. The gate attendants enforce the rules as strictly or leniently as they wish. I have seen people carrying full-sized duffels without detention at the gate. Camera bags, computer laptops, binoculars, handbags, briefcases, shopping bags, daypacks, garment bags, and duty-free bags all count toward the two-bag carry-on limit. During all my travels, with my 3500 cubic-inch bag as a carry-on, I had trouble only one time. After waiting two days in the Senegal airport for a flight out, I learned that an "empty" Swissair 747 would stop for me and two other passengers, but they said that all our carry-ons exceeded size limits. I refused to give up my bag because I thought this sounded like a joke. After several comments back and forth, the airport manager allowed the bags on board.

You need to adjust to strange situations in remote parts of the world. If I travel for several weeks, I check heavy and/or bulky items like tent, mosquito net, sleeping bag, hiking boots, cooking equipment, and prepackaged foods. If I still needed to use these items, I would avoid checking any bags. I learned a difficult lesson after checking a water purifier in my luggage on a trip to Ethiopia. It was not until I needed the purifier in the first remote village on my itinerary that I realized the airlines somehow broke the handle, making the purifier useless. I counted on that piece of equipment for a month-long journey in areas without bottled water. The airlines bought me a new purifier after I returned, a little late for my purposes.

Carry-on bags should lock tightly so that loose articles do not make their way out either by falling or by sneaky fingers.

Airlines allow some items not included in the two-piece carry-on limit like coats, umbrellas, canes or crutches, reading materials, and diaper bags.

Prohibited items in checked or carry-on bags may include flammables, tear gas, any type of fuel cylinders or refills with gas, kerosene or butane, and weapons of any type.

Aerosols, lighters, and solvents will not survive the search, so leave them at home. Coming back from Addis Ababa, Ethiopia, the thorough body search targeted cigarette lighters. In today's climate of terrorism searches, the list of prohibited items expands.

TSA's carry-on security measure requires liquids in 3.4-ounce (100ml) bottles or less. They allow these to be carried in only a one-quart sized, clear, zip-top bag per passenger. If unsure about an item, check it. I bought a 500ml bottle of coconut massage oil in Bali and found some small plastic vinegar bottles at the market to transfer the oil into after dumping all the vinegar into a water bottle for the owner of the store. He loved getting the free vinegar. I packed eight tiny bottles plus my other six small bottles of liquids. Security told me to either check the stuff or throw it away. I knew the airlines would charge twenty-five dollars for the first bag checked, so I threw the ten-dollar oil away.

Carry-on emphasizes mobility and freedom. Saving time in the baggage claim area, keeping your luggage within reach (and not on its way to Timbuktu), and not needing to lay money on porters to help you maneuver several bags, make using carry-on luggage worthwhile.

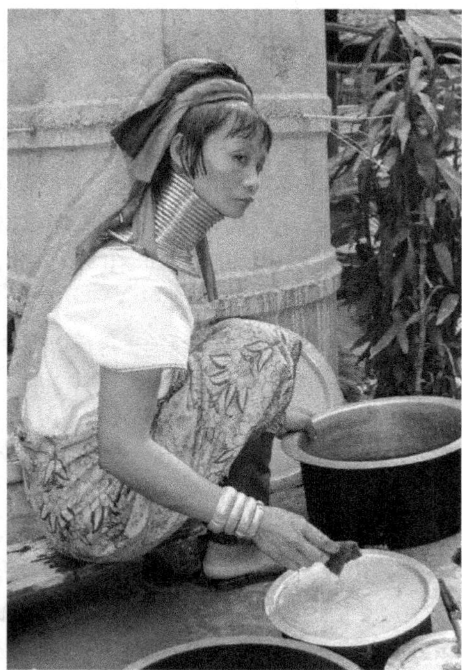

*19. Giraffe-neck woman cleaning cooking pots, Thailand*

### BAGGAGE ALLOWANCES

Airlines differ throughout the world on international baggage limitations, and you may find it hard to inquire about internal flights within a country before you go, a critical factor for packing. The general rule for foreign-based international flights equals twenty kg., about forty-four pounds of luggage, total per person. Tiny intra-country airlines limit weights to fifteen kg. The weight total for American-based airlines will range from fifty to seventy pounds total for checking, and the rule relates to weight limits, not quantity of bags. Carry-on bags must not exceed individual requirements, which differ with each airline. I cannot tell you how many times I have had to repack my carry-on bag in front of the ticket agent for international flights after they weighed my carry-on bag. The five kg. or eleven lb. limit adds up fast with cameras, computers, and books. The airlines have the right to refuse carry-ons weighing over five kg., even if they might fit under a seat. Keep in mind that, although not all airlines enforce the limitations, you must prepare for that occasional by-the-book ticket agent.

Flights from North America have a different set of rules. Most airlines allow passengers two pieces of luggage checked per person, but read the rules in small print when making a reservation. Weight and size limits vary by airline. This means that your through fare from Kansas City to Timbuktu allows you two pieces of luggage all the way. However, if you pay one fare from Kansas City/London/Bamako and then an additional fare from Bamako to Timbuktu on Fun Africa Airlines, then for that last portion you will have the weight limit of forty-four lbs. total. In most cases, you will not buy a through-fare to points in South Asia and Africa and small cities in South America. Schedules and costs change all the time, and online sites do not show local airline information. Most airlines now charge for checked luggage with each varying in price. Airlines post their checked baggage rates on their web sites.

### EXCESS BAGGAGE

Airlines do not need to accept excess baggage at all. Small airlines sometimes will refuse all excess baggage. Airlines base acceptance of excess luggage on a stand-by basis. This means the luggage may travel on a later flight. The charges vary, so a phone call to the airline will answer how much. The cost of shipping as unaccompanied luggage far exceeds the charges for excess luggage. Airfreight or air cargo charges cost more per pound per mile, and airlines make more money on cargo than passengers. Your luggage, including overweight bags, can go through customs, but freight or cargo shipped as unaccompanied can take weeks to clear customs unless you pay expensive expediting fees or bribes. This fact explains why courier companies need individuals to accompany their packages through customs.

### *CLOTHES*

You can buy most clothes upon arrival in foreign countries if you forget something or would prefer to fit in with the locals. Except for expensive countries like Japan, you can get clothing cheap, but it lacks quality. I buy most of my travel clothing from travel catalogs, camping stores, and sporting goods stores. There you will find fabrics using the latest technology for wicking moisture, blocking the sun's rays, and quick washing and drying. Hidden pockets, plus extra pockets with secure closures, appear as added features in travel clothing. Clothing will last through many trips if kept only for traveling. I predict you will love these items so much, you will find yourself wearing them at home. Look for double duty items like pants that zip off the lower section for conversion to shorts or sarongs for use as beach towels You can use sheets on a train bench, and skirts or scarves to enter temples, or to cover up while bathing in a river. Take a long tee shirt for a beach cover-up or for sleeping.

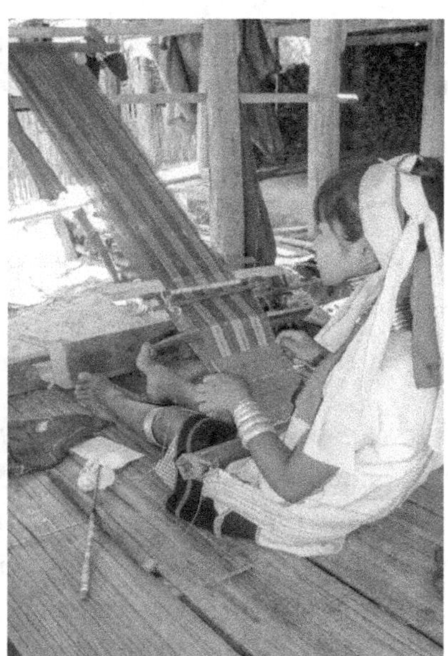

*20. Girl with back strap loom, Thailand*

### SHOES

Do not leave home without your most comfortable, tried, and loved pair of shoes. When traveling, you will appreciate comfortable shoes more than any other item packed. Avoiding tired, aching feet far outweighs showing off those shiny (but stiff) new hiking boots. Plan far in advance which shoes you must take on your journey. What about those hiking boots stored away in your winter closet? About six weeks before a trip, I pull out my boots and start wearing them every day, everywhere. Yes, I get some strange looks when I show up with my children at ski club practice in my bathing suit and hiking boots. Do not worry about getting your favorite pair dirty or worn out. Just buy a new pair when you get back.

Athletic shoes and hiking boots from the United States serve as a status symbol in other countries. Often you will have men approach you asking you to give or sell them your shoes. Shopping for shoes abroad calls for an added expense for superior quality, and then you have the breaking in period. In Third and Fourth World Countries, you will see rubber sandals or flip-flops/thongs. Plastic thongs sell for around three dollars in markets everywhere. Use them for showers, crossing rivers, or walking in the sand. They will not last long walking in mud, so buy quality Tevas before leaving home if you plan to wear that type of shoe for any length of time. Whatever you take, make sure you break it in. Blisters can cause a nuisance in tropical temperatures. They can take weeks to heal, develop infections, and disrupt your walking plans.

### TIPS FOR PACKING

If you worry about clothing items wrinkling, wrap them in dry cleaner bags before folding. Folding clothes in half and then rolling helps to prevent wrinkles. Use fabric softener sheets in your luggage to keep clothes smelling fresh. These sheets cut down on static cling also. Put socks and undergarments inside shoes/boots to save space. An attractive jewelry case doubles as a purse. Leave the heavy everyday purse or wallet at home. Reduce your wallet size by taking one or two credit cards and leave the rest of the business and membership cards that have no use on the road.

Tear old destination baggage tags off your luggage before you leave so your luggage will not arrive at the wrong place. Wear dark clothes that will not show spots while traveling. Pack double the number of your own personal business cards you think you will need. They establish credibility and assure you a professional statement.

Place heavy items like shoes near the end of luggage with wheels. Place weatherproof items (like ponchos) on top for quick rainstorms. A poncho can double as a bag protector.

A bike lock makes a useful tethering lock for train stations, bus depots, table legs, etc. for added security.

Hide and secure jewelry, and small, fragile items in an empty soap container. Rubber bands keep socks and shoes together.

Repair a broken zipper, luggage tag or missing button with a twist tie, cable tie, or safety pin.

A deck of cards or game of UNO can alleviate boredom during long layovers from flat tires or weather delays.

Buy small three-inch square Ziploc bags at drug stores for storage of pills, saving tons of space by removing pills from pharmacy/vitamin bottles. Count out extras for emergencies instead of taking entire bottles. Minimize containers and bottles and use Ziploc bags. Two-gallon bags, marked with permanent marker or labels, make handy storage bags for underwear, socks, and miscellaneous items.

Wrap a two-foot piece of duct tape around a pencil for emergency repair to luggage handles or broken shoe straps. Create rain boots by placing plastic bags over your shoes and secure them with rubber bands.

# Chapter 16: customs and going home

*"Follow your bliss and the universe will open doors for you where there were only walls."* Joseph Campbell

***CUSTOMS***

Customs should not slow you down if you understand the procedure. After you make your way through the sometimes-long lines in immigration, the customs officer will see you. He may or may not ask you where you have traveled, why, and for how long. He may ask if you have any agricultural items and then will look at your declarations form, given to you by the airline host to fill out before landing. He will look for illegal items not allowed in the country and/or dutiable items acquired while traveling. If you have film in your camera, it may be ruined, for customs will sometimes search your luggage, and open your camera back. This is another reason to go digital.

Do not accept any packages from recent friends in foreign countries to deliver in the United States as these packages may contain drugs. Customs officials levy a duty or tax on certain legal items you bring into the country with you. You have an allowance for a certain amount to spend on personal purchases.

When you leave on your trip, you can register valuables like cameras, computers, etc. at the airport. The registration certificate will prove you brought the items with you upon departure, and you will not have to pay duty on them when returning.

I have never been charged duty on these types of items and do not recommend taking the time to register your items before leaving the country, but it certainly can't hurt.

Keep all sales receipts of purchases in one place, as you must show them to customs upon returning if they ask for them. I have never had to show my receipts.

***GOING HOME***

Travel equals the best education you can get. By mastering the currency, trying some local food, learning a few words of the local language, meeting and making new foreign friends, you will learn so much about a new culture. As a side benefit, this will help you understand your own country better because you will see it from another point of view. Until you take root in another culture, you do not realize your own capabilities. When all those take-for-granteds disappear in a foreign country, you begin to appreciate their importance. Day-to-day structure disappears as you travel, and you soon miss those humdrum routines of life at home.

Adventure travel requires meeting with challenges and risks. The real danger occurs when your eyes open to diversity and discoveries about the real world. Cultural interaction arouses global understanding. Moreover, with global understanding comes world peace. By allowing the foreignness of a place to encircle you, you can narrow your panoramic view of your place in the world. You gain a clear perspective of your life, friends, and job. After that first stamp appears on your passport, nothing will ever remain the same again.

Do not push yourself when you return home. In order to make your old world your own again, acclimate yourself one day at a time. Living in the desert with one change of clothing over a period of several weeks causes a mild shock when opening a closet door back home. Culture shock intensifies when you return home after having traveled to Third and Fourth World countries. When discussing travel, my family still remarks, "Mom and Katherine never did come back from their trip to New Guinea."

When you return, your mind finds the time to think about what you have seen while your body wants to accustom itself to old habits. Read your journal, take long walks, and listen to your favorite music in the park. Unwind. Food will surface as abundant and lavish. You will want to overindulge. After returning from poor countries, I often feel I owe donuts and pizza to myself, since I gave them up for a month. Naturally, I gain weight. Donuts and pizza never find my kitchen before a trip, but their unavailability on a trip intensifies my cravings for them when I return. Remember to make slow and gentle adjustments for your digestive system after returning home.

A hunger develops for relationships almost the minute you return home. Coming home forces you to confront those familiar people and things. The transformations you have undergone, and the stress of those confrontations, make it impossible to find your old self again.

Thousands of items line shelves in grocery stores, unlike the small markets of undeveloped villages. Ashamed of thinking I need so much, I stay away from the grocery store the first week after my return. Your interaction with new social forces from foreign travel produces new customs and traditions. You push into change, but this helps you appreciate the things you do not want to change. You gain a new perspective on life, which in turn, helps you reestablish priorities.

Things like driving home on the highway from the airport will seem alien to you. I remember how hard it was to open my closet after being in New Guinea for a month. I did not want to look at all those shoes on the floor of my closet. I found out that my one pair of shoes served me well, and yes, friends still tell me how boring I am because I wear the same shoes every day. The Dani people wore no clothing or shoes, knew nothing of jealousy or competition or dishonesty, and looked like the happiest people I have ever met. The choices we have overpower the meek existence of those living in underdeveloped places. Simplify your home life while you adjust to demands from friends and business.

Felix Marti-Ibanez once said, "There is one priceless thing that I brought back from my trip around the world, one that cost no money and on which I paid no customs duty: humility, a humility born from watching other peoples, other races, struggling bravely and hoping humbly for the simplest things in life."

My daughter Katherine (fourteen at the time) soaked up the contented lifestyle of the Dani the way a dry sponge soaks up water. Her materialistic teenage world of music, make-up, and boys took second place to her life's dreams; she yearned for a taste of that simpler living without the diversions of the American dream. On her own, she found friends in Ecuador who invited her to live with them while she finished high school, and later she went on to college at the University of the Andes. She has developed a compassionate understanding of the world and its people like no one I have ever met.

Intimate experiences with foreign cultures take the traveler beyond the surface of their normal lives. Replacing home familiarity with new, in-depth, thought-provoking opportunities gives us new meaning to our lives. Preoccupation with a new culture can get into your blood.

Self-discovery from travel changes people. Your friends and loved ones expect you to arrive home as the same person you were when you left. This causes most people to fall into their old patterns upon returning home. Your friends do not want to get to know someone new, but you want to share what you have experienced. Soon your friends realize they cannot understand the magnitude of the change. Trying to explain this to your friends may disrupt their lives.

Jealousy is a common reaction for those who recognize your new-found self. You will notice that everything is the same as when you left, and people will want you to get into the same old grind. The same responsibilities and problems still await your responses. If, because of your travels, you grow more independent and determined, then this changes the whole system. Everyone else has to change to meet your new needs. This can lead to depression on the part of your family and friends, or, at the least, some resistance to your new attitudes.

Why travel? Part of the answer involves the challenge, and the fear of the unknown.

I ask people I meet in my travels why they ended up "here." Time after time, the answer is the same. The tiniest trickle of suspense, like in a good book, keeps travelers going. In this book that does not have all the answers, there lies a search for what is over the next hill. Why travel if you know all the answers? If your travel plans did not include some forms of challenges, there would exist no self-satisfaction in facing them. Once you allow the journey to take you, something happens that, in the beginning, caused your greatest fear.

Without the habitual routines, and the presence of those you love surrounding you, you grow self-reliant from your own decisions, weaknesses, and strengths.

In each new situation, your challenges stretch your limits. Unfamiliar territories demand common sense, leaving you with a sense of appreciation for the world and the life you left behind. Whether you heard the call of the spirit winds, held a winning lottery ticket, discovered your own self-motivation, or responded as your mother pushed you out into the world, the past path will cease to remain the decisive factor. Instead of your dreams, scattering in the wind, you took a journey into yourself, strengthening a positive sense of self.

# Chapter 17: resource list one: reference

***REFERENCE BOOKS/PUBLICATIONS***

From the Superintendent of Documents, U.S. Government Printing Office, Washington, D.C. 20402, you may obtain many publications for $1.25.

Examples include "Your Trip Abroad," "Safe Trip Abroad," "Tips for Americans Residing Abroad," "Travel Tips for Older Americans," and many publications on specific parts of the world like "Tips for Travelers to the Caribbean."

*Background Notes* offer you detailed information about a particular foreign country.

Each booklet contains information on 170 different countries and geographic areas with descriptions of people, culture, geography, history, political conditions, economy, and government.

Include the specific country or area you plan to visit, and $2 with your request to Background Notes, Superintendent of Documents, U.S. Government Printing Office, Washington D.C. 20402, or check the web site at www.state.gov.

*Key Officers of Foreign Service Posts* booklet has valuable information on all American Embassies, consulates, and missions in foreign countries including names, addresses, and telephone numbers for $3.75.

Use the same address as *Background Notes* (above) or call 202-783-3238.

***CUSTOMS***

"Know Before You Go" Booklet available free from the U.S. Customs Service, Box74077, Washington, DC 20044

"Travelers Tips on Bringing Food, Plant, and Animal Products into the United States" is free from the U.S. Department of Agriculture, Washington, D.C. 20250

***EMERGENCIES***

To find travel information for emergencies, consider the following website: www.travel.state.gov.

Overseas Citizen Emergency Center will help with any legal, financial, or medical problems occurring while abroad.

They will help notify relatives at home, help with medical support, or help you receive money. Their hotline provides information on entry requirements, crime and security conditions, and areas of instability related to travel for a particular country.

They issue travel warnings when the State Department recommends deferral of travel by Americans to a country because of civil unrest, dangerous conditions or terrorist conditions, and when the U.S. has no diplomatic relations with the country or cannot assist Americans in distress.

The Policy Review and Interagency Liaison (PRI) Agency provides guidance concerning the administration and enforcement of laws on U.S. citizenship and documentation for traveling and living abroad for Americans. Reach them at this same number.

The State Department's Office of American Citizens Services and Crisis Management (ACS) office administers the Consular Information Program, which informs the public of conditions abroad that may affect their safety and security. Useful information includes Country Specific Information, Travel Alerts, and Travel Warnings.

To contact Overseas Citizens Services from within the U.S, call 1-888-407-4747 and from a foreign country call 1-202-501-4444, or write Overseas Citizens Services Department of State Washington, DC 20520, or find the online site at:

www.travel.state.gov/travel/travel_1744.html.

Global Assist can help American Express Card members. They have a free hot-line to assist with medical, legal, translation and professional problems. In the US, the phone number is 800-333-AMEX and abroad, call collect at 715-343-7977.

### *FREIGHTER TRAVEL*

If you plan to visit the Panama and the Suez canals, you're going to have to spend a considerable amount of time at sea, since the Panama Canal is in the Western Hemisphere, and the Suez Canal is in the Middle East.

Try checking out Maris Freighter & Specialty Cruises (www.freighter-cruises.com, or toll-free, 800-99-Maris) offers a 15-week voyage that includes both canals, but it begins and ends outside of the United States. Trips sail every month from Dunkirk to Le Havre, France, then across the Atlantic to Cristobal, Panama, and through the Panama Canal to Tahiti, then on to New Zealand, New Caledonia, Fiji, Vanuatu, the Solomon Islands, Papua, New Guinea, and then to Singapore, followed by a passage through the Suez Canal and the Mediterranean, ending in Hamburg, Germany.

The same company also offers an eastbound cruise starting and ending in Texas.

This voyage lasts 18 weeks. The itinerary starts in Texas, moves up the East Coast of the United States, and then includes Hamburg, Germany, Belgium, Italy, the Suez Canal, India, Indonesia, Singapore, Vietnam, various ports in China, Korea, Japan. The return to the States, stopps in Southern California, passing through the Panama Canal, and ending in Houston, Texas.

For a variation check out Strand Voyages: See www.strandtravelltd.co.uk/voyages/destinations-and-prices/

Freighter World: www.freighterworld.com/ or 800-531-7774

TravL tips: www.travltips.com or 800-872-8584; Freighter trips for tips and info: http://www.freightertrips.com/.

### *GEAR*

Campmor 1-800-525-4784 or www.campmor.com.

Magellans 1-800-962-494 or www.magellans.com.

Sierra Trading Post 800-713-4534 or www.sierraTradingPost.com.

Travel Smith 800-770-3387 or www.travelsmith.com

REI 1-800-426-4840 or www.rei.com

Columbia Clothing www.columbia.com

Ex Officio 800-644-7303 or www.exofficio.com

### *INSURANCE*

Insure My Trip 800-551-4635 or www.insuremytrip.com

Global Travel Shield 1-800-332-4899 or www.globaltravelshield.com

Travel Guard 800.826.4919 or www.travelguard.com

Assess America 800.826.4919 or www.assessamerica.com

CIEE (Council on International Educational Exchange) 1-207-553-4000 or www.ciee.org.

Healthcare Abroad 800-237-6615 or www.wallach.com.

International SOS Assistance is helpful at www.internationalsos.com.

Travel Trip (Mutual of Omaha) 800-228-9792

Travel Assistance International 800-237-6615; www.travelassistance.com.

***MEDICAL CONCERNS***

Center for Disease Control (if your doctor or local public health department cannot answer your questions or problems with medical matters) 800-CDC-INFO or www.cdc.gov..

IAMAT International Association for Medical Assistance to Travelers 716 -754 -4883

Alternatively, check out www.iamat.org. This organization keeps an up-to-date chart of all the diseases and malaria for every country in the world.

When you figure out where you plan to travel, you can go to this website, find the world immunization chart, and find your destination country.

Each disease active in that country has a code. Look further down the chart to see whether you need immunizations for that country. The chart gives advice on the best drugs to use and how much and when to take them.

I found my general doctor did not know much about malaria, and I used the IAMAT advice to help him determine how much medicine to prescribe.

If you join their organization, they send a little booklet with recommended doctors for every country in the world listed.

I found this information invaluable when my fourteen-year-old daughter came down with malaria symptoms while we traipsed through the New Guinea jungles.

As soon as we arrived in a town large enough to have a hospital and doctor, we found the doctor recommended in the little book.

Katherine and I loved the attention he gave us, including a ride to the pharmacy to help with translating his prescription, and then to our hotel to make sure Katherine found comfort for the night.

***STUDENT TRAVEL ORGANIZATIONS***

Council on International Education Exchange (CIEE) A nonprofit organization helping with work, study, exchange and travel abroad 1-207-553-4000 or www.ciee.org.

Student Travel Association (STA) 800-781-4040 or www.statravel.com

International Student Volunteers www.isvonline.com.

National Registration Center for Study Abroad 414-278-0631 or www.nrcsa.com.

Hosteling International www.hihostels.com.

### TRAVEL ORGANIZATIONS for SINGLES

www.BestSingleTravel.com.
www.Travelchums.com
www.TravelCompanionExchange.com
www.SinglesTravelCompany.com 888.286.8687
www.AllSinglesTravel.com 888.286.8687
www.SoloTravel.org

### TRAVEL ORGANIZATIONS FOR SENIORS

My Travel Companions (free membership to find travel companions for seniors) www.mytravelcompanions.com

American Association of Retired Persons (AARP) www.aarp.org/travel
www.RoadScholar.org 888.286.8687
www.Eldertreks.com 800-741-7956

### TRAVEL WARNINGS, REVIEWS, ADVICE WEBSITES

Consular Information Sheets and Travel Warnings 202-647-5225. You can obtain warnings at passport agencies, US embassies and consulates abroad, or access them through the Consular Affairs Bulletin Board (CABB) free. Request by fax at 202-647-3000. For each country, you will find information such as the location of the U.S. embassy and any consular offices, whether you need a visa, or seek crime and security warnings.

When friends or family of an American traveler need to reach him or her because of an emergency at home or because they are worried about the traveler's welfare, they should call 1-888-407-4747.

For emergencies, contact the Office of Overseas Citizens Services in the U.S. at 1-888-407-4747 (during business hours) or 202-647-5225 (after hours).

Contact information for U.S. embassies, consulates, and you may also contact U.S. consular agencies overseas: www.state.gov/countries.

www.Advisor.com offers reviews and advice on everything related to travel, including hotels.

www.VirtualTourist.com offers advice and answers from people who have traveled your destination.

www.LonelyPlanet.com/ThornTree offers a place to ask questions and get advice on all elements of travel.

Join travel blogs like www.travelblogs.org. Check the browser for the most popular as they change constantly.

www.JackieChase.com updates this book + has tips/ideas for the traveler.

# Chapter 18: resource list two: lists

***CARRY-ON PACKING LIST***

>Photocopies of all documents in a separate Ziploc bag

>Camera, memory cards, appropriate batteries, film as needed

>Ziploc for 3 oz. liquids and basic toiletries

>IPod, iPad, or other device for listening to music, watching movies

>Laptop for email, travel research

>Medications [Include prescription- and side-effect information]

>Reading glasses, spare glasses, and/or sunglasses with neck string or croakies

>Lead bag for holding photographic film

>Travel organizer, journal, magazines, and at least five pens

>Paperback books you can trade after you have read them on the trip

>Luggage and brass lock, keys, nail clipper for cable ties

>All fragile items like breakable water purifiers

>Money belt or waist belt

>Flashlight

>Maps and Xeroxed copies from guide books to study while traveling

***STANDARD LIST FOR THREE-WEEK ADVENTURE TRIP***

[This does not include clothing or items worn on the plane.]

>Two pairs of pants, one with zip-off legs to convert to shorts for remote trips

>Two long-sleeve shirts

>One short-sleeve shirt

>One tee and leggings for sleeping

>[For women: A long skirt or a sarong that doubles as a skirt; three bras, three panties (silk dries in an hour)]

>[For men: Briefs with polyester in them (dry faster for hand washing than 100% cotton)]

>Swimsuit

>Packable towel, made for traveling, available at TravelSmith, Magellans, CampMor, Etc. [They work like a small chamois and dry in about an hour in the tropics.]

>Wear the boots. Pack flip-flops and comfortable walking or tennis shoes

>Rain jacket or rain poncho and rain pants if weather suggests

>Handful of rubber bands

>Fleece shirt or jacket

>Water purifier and water purification tablets in case the purifier breaks while traveling [you can find bottled water most everywhere.]

>Hat

>Wear watch with an alarm or take a small travel alarm

>Three pair of Thorlo type socks (see travel catalogs) or socks with polyester for fast drying.

>Snacks for each day such as beef jerky, cheese sticks, nuts, power bars/protein bars and packets of peanut butter.

>Waist pouch for needed essentials like sunglasses, map and a little spending money

>Flat money pouch with waist strap for wearing inside your clothing [for all documents, rest of money and air tickets]

>First Aid Kit

>Belt [wear it]

>Twenty-foot length of small rope for clothesline or to tie a bag together if zipper breaks

>Several safety pins to hang clothes to dry and to hold things together if they break

>A needle with a long piece of thread attached to repair a broken zipper, etc. or as a tool to dig out splinters

>Extra sets of batteries for flashlight, camera, or flash. For areas with electricity, use rechargeable batteries. With the charger, take eight rechargeable batteries

***LIST OF BASIC TOILETRIES***

Pack in two, one-gallon size, Ziploc bags; Take ONLY necessary items

>Deodorant

>Two razors

>Bar of soap in plastic traveling soap container

>Toothbrush in plastic container, toothpaste (3 oz. size), dental floss

>Hairbrush and/or comb

>Facial products

>Shampoo/conditioner in 3 oz. bottles (separate into quart size Ziploc for security)

>Sunscreen (separate into quart-size Ziploc for security)

>Lip balm like Blistex

>Women: menstrual supplies, minimal cosmetics, and expendable jewelry

>Condoms, birth control supplies

>Eye care

>Make up (separate into quart size Ziploc for security)

>Two large safety pins

>One nylon adhesive patch for rips in bags, raincoats, and tents

***CAMPING LIST***

>Waterproof tent with shock cord poles

>Sleeping bag, insulated for your type of trip

>Water bottle, flat-when-empty type, like the Platypus Brand, works well for packing

>Self-inflating sleeping pad

>Cooking stove that uses a fuel available where you travel

>Matches

>Cooking equipment necessary for your type of travel

>Dehydrated, canned, or prepackaged food

>Space blanket

***LIST OF ADDITIONAL BASICS*** (Depends on particular interests)

>Binoculars

>Snorkel, mask, fins

>Gore-Tex hiking boots

>Whistle, pepper spray, or mace (check with TSA: might need to buy in a foreign country)

>Deck of cards, small games, notepad, crossword puzzles, art supplies, etc.

>Hammock

>Mosquito net with equipment to hang (string and tiny nails) and repellent with DEET

>Global positioning system

>Tripod, video camera, recorder

>Waterproof containers for documents and camera while swimming or raining

***LIST OF BASICS FOR COLD CLIMATES***

>Insulated underwear (either silk, polypropylene, or new fabric that wicks moisture but holds in heat)

>Wool or combination polypropylene socks for warmth, with liners for additional warmth made from the newer fabrics that hold in heat but not moisture.

>Waterproof socks if necessary

>Clothing useful when layered. Fleece shells/pants/neck wraps/face masks

>Fleece or wool hat

>Insulated gloves made for extreme temperatures. Glove liners, made from nylon, polyester, or silk combinations help with protection

>Packets of heat that are shaken or rubbed to activate, then inserted into gloves or socks [try to find ones that heat for eight hours or more]

>Appropriate type of jacket (down filled and/or Gore-tex)

***BASIC FIRST AID KIT LIST***

>Ibuprofen and/or Tylenol, or with codeine for pain

>Prescription antibiotics for infections

>Band-Aids (3 or 4 cloth versions: hold better than plastic), gauze (few pieces), tape (roll some duct tape around a pencil)

>Hydrocortisone cream, Antifungal cream, Neosporin or Bacitracin (Neosporin causes itching for many people.)

>Imodium and Pepto-Bismol tablets

>Moleskin/gel packs and foam pads for blisters (not entire packet just a couple)

>Wrist bracelet, patches, or motion sickness tablets (enough for the trip)

>Individual packets of tissue (one packet for every two days)

>Individual packets of disinfectant hand wipes (one for each day) or hand sanitizer

>Vitamins

>Cold pills, flu and/or allergy tablets (might use these types of pills, which cause drowsiness, for help with sleeping in noisy places or when a guide shares your hut and snores)

>Prescribed medicines for diseases found in areas of travel (e.g. malaria: some TSA agents will ask to see a prescription for a drug even though the drug is in a bottle with label on it. If it is necessary, get a note from a doctor. Agents could take away children's medications)

>Photo copies of health facts from guide books (probable diseases, illnesses from the destination)

>List other items specific to the age and condition of the traveler and the special challenges of the destinations

***LIST FOR LONGER OR SURVIVAL TYPE TRIP***

>Ace bandage, Breathe-Right strips, toilet paper, alcohol, foot powder, superglue for cuts or butterfly bandages, snake suction kit, blank CD disk for signal mirror, whistle (because people get hoarse when lost and calling for help), map, compass, and a small Ziploc with some denture cream squirted inside (a crown or filling can be glued back in temporarily.)

***DOCUMENT LIST***

>Passport

>Visa

>International vaccination certificate

>U.S. money

>Travelers' checks

>One or two credit cards

>Airline ticket or email information with flights and times and confirmation numbers

>Address and phone numbers of close friends and family

>Driver's license, if driving while traveling; international, if needed

***LIST OF OTHER TO-DOS BEFORE LEAVING HOME*** (Reverse on return)

>Call credit card company and tell them where you will be traveling and for how long

>Immunizations

>Put a hold on mail, paper and other services

>Arrange for a phone and/or card used internationally

>Make arrangements for pets and houseplants

>Arrange for someone to take care of yard

>Set up automatic payment for mortgage, utilities, etc.

>Move some money from savings into credit cards or checking account or lower your credit card limit for protection if your card is stolen

>Leave a copy of your itinerary and maps with a friend or neighbor

>Print double the amount of business cards you think you will need. (They will establish credibility and arm you with a professional statement about yourself if needed. For business travelers, have all your business information printed on the back of your card in the language of the country you visit.)

>Adjust thermostat to save energy on utilities and turn the hot water heater to "Vacation" or "Off."

>Close all blinds, curtains

>Unplug large appliances like stoves, televisions, and computers

>Turn water off to the house or shut valves to toilets and washing machines

>Set timers with various lights and radio to go on at night for a few hours

***Bon Voyage!***

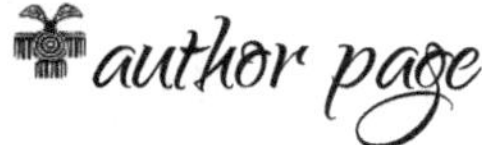

Jackie Chase, [www.JackieChase.com, www.WorldTravelDiva.com, and www.CulturesOfTheWorld.com], has traveled to over 100 countries and specializes in staying in remote villages in order to use her keen observations and photo-journalism skills to share her insights with her reader fans. She has traveled alone, with a child, with family, and with friends; she has earned 29 awards from international book contests from 2014 to date of printing; she shares with the public many of the travel secrets she has experienced in her book titled, ***"How to Become an Escape Artist" A Traveler's Handbook.*** The Handbook was tested for several years with students in a college evening class, and they soaked up Jackie's hints and the many ways to avoid disappointment, reduce expenses and frustrations, navigate the issues of visas, language, customs, currencies, accommodations, transportation, attitudes, danger, travel alone, and other problems all covered in over 190 segments in the book.

Her ***"All Hands Working Together" Cruise for a Week: Meet 79 Cultures*** book treats cruising in a unique way to learn about cultures; the reader experiences personal contact with crewmembers from many of the 79 countries they represent, and from many skills they possess.

Jackie Chase has written definitive books on "People to Meet" in contrast to "Places to See". She convinces her readership to look beyond mountains, lakes and buildings to see world inhabitants of all continents as potential friends and shows how much we have in common. She shows how to bridge gaps created by custom and language in ***"100 People to Meet before You Die: Travel to Exotic Places".*** This book, [as well as the others], are available in color, grayscale, and, with stunning images in eBooks that come to life on backlit screens. This anthology contains 321 of those story-telling images ward-winning prose about her adventures in twelve countries. For her fans of a particular country, she has twelve "singles" in print and in eBook format, plus at least one (Panama) translated into Spanish.

For children, from small up through teens, a "winner" of a book is ***"Giraffe-Neck Girl" Make Friends with Different Cultures.*** It is about a ten-year-old girl in Thailand who warms the hearts of young and old as she shares her different life and customs.

Jackie Chase's 2016 book, ***"Walking to Woot" A Photographic Narrative Discovering New Dimensions for Parent-Teen Bonding*** has won 15 international awards in the genres of Parenting, Multi-Cultural, and Travel, and it contains both poetic descriptions and visual ones with its 180 images of life with stone-age tribal warriors who haven't changed customs in a thousand years. The New

Guinea unclothed villagers welcomed Jackie and her blond 14-year-old daughter to pig roasts, unusual customs, and dances. Jackie Chase loves to hear from her fans and to see copies of reviews they submit to the web. Contact her:

JakartaMoon@hotmail.com, or Publisher@AdventureTravelPress.com.

These adventures in 12 countries are available on the web as singles, beginning with the name of the country, and this book is available in print with stunning black and white or color images through web book distributors such as: www.AdventureTravelPress.com, or Kindle, Ingram, Amazon, and Nook.

In electronic download form, these, and other books by the author, can be ordered from all e-book sources. Images from this and other books are available for framing in many sizes upon request. Ask for the catalogue at: Publisher@AdventureTravelPress.com.

***BOOKS BY JACKIE CHASE: 2014/17***

*All Hands Working Together: Cruise for a Week: Meet 79 Cultures (2014-6)*
*How to Become an Escape Artist: A Traveler's Handbook (2014-6) Giraffe-Neck Girl: Make Friends with a Different Culture (2014)*
*100 People to Meet before You Die: Travel to Exotic Cultures (2014-6)*

***AWARDS (14) FOR THE FOUR BOOKS LISTED ABOVE*** Royal Palm Literary Award; National Indie Excellence Book Award;
FAPA President's Book Award; Readers' Favorite Book Award; International Book Award; USA Best Book Award; Beverly Hills Book Awards

***AWARDS (15) For:*** "*Walking to Woot*" A Photographic Narrative Discovering New Dimensions for Parent-Teen Bonding

Beach Book Festival; Beverly Hills Book Awards in 3 Categories; Eric Hoffer Grand Prize Awards in 2 Categories; Florida Authors and Publishers Association (FAPA); International Book Award, Montaigne Medals; National Indie Excellence Award; Next Generation Indie Book Awards in 2 Categories; Paris Book Festival; Reader's Favorite Awards in 2 Categories; San Francisco Festival Awards.

All books (including 13 "smaller single-country books" in English, and some in Spanish) available at: www.AdventureTravelPress.com
Traveler notes and ideas: